This book is intended (a) as an introduction for those who do not already know Pannenberg's theology, and (b) to discuss some of the problems which it presents for those who do.

Pannenberg's theology of history has already been widely discussed. This is the first work to treat his theology as a whole — his doctrine of man, of history, of God and the Trinity, of christology and resurrection, of church and eschatology — showing how it all hangs together. It presents Pannenberg's work sympathetically, but not uncritically. Criticisms which others have made are discussed and some new ones offered. The exposition is creative, offering fresh interpretations and, occasionally, venturing to suggest possible improvements in Pannenberg's presentation of his argument. It is thus an original contribution as well as an interpretation.

This book is directed to that growing section of the public which likes to keep in touch with what is happening in the forefront of theology, and to know where the growth points are. Theological students will find it a useful aid to their own reading of Pannenberg.

The author is a distinguished Scottish theologian with wide experience of interpreting contemporary continental theology.

WOLFHART PANNENBERG

CONTEMPORARY
RELIGIOUS THINKERS SERIES
Edited by H. D. Lewis

WOLFHART PANNENBERG

Allan D. Galloway
Professor of Divinity, University of Glasgow

London · George Allen & Unwin Ltd
Ruskin House   Museum Street

First published 1973

ISBN: 0 04 230011 8 hardback
ISBN: 0 04 230012 6 paperback

Printed in Great Britain
in 12 point Fournier
by The Aldine Press
Letchworth · Herts

General Editor's Note on the Series

This series sets out to provide a critical assessment of the work of some of the most notable and influential religious thinkers of today. It is intended mainly for students and laymen seriously interested in the study of religion. The authors will vary in the degree of their own sympathy with the thinkers they discuss, and scope will be given to them to make a distinctive contribution of their own to the topics they examine.

The writers discussed in the series will include, in addition to informative thinkers in Europe and the Western world, some notable Eastern writers of today. There will thus be made available to our readers some instructive critical comment on writers with whom they may not otherwise have much acquaintance.

Contents

PANNENBERG

Born in 1928, Wolfhart Pannenberg is one of the most distinguished of the new generation of German theologians. He studied theology under Karl Barth in Basel in 1950. In 1951 he went to Heidelberg where, with a group of other research students, he played a leading part in what is sometimes still known as the Pannenberg circle. It was this group which brought forth the volume *Revelation as History* which Pannenberg edited. This early work is the key to much that has happened since. After the completion of his doctoral studies he became a lecturer in Heidelberg. He became Professor of Systematic Theology in a church Seminary at Wuppertal in 1958. In 1961 he was appointed to the chair of Systematic Theology in Mainz. Since 1968 he has held the same chair in Munich.

He made his first impact at the end of the era dominated by the three giants Barth, Bultmann and Tillich. For them critical history raised problems. For Pannenberg it provided answers. This new relationship between historical research and systematic theology, whereby history becomes a source of confidence rather than doubt and theology becomes the source of a credible philosophy of history, marks a profound change in the whole direction and ethos of theology.

It has changed the shape of all the traditional issues of theology —the relation between transcendence and immanence, the sacred and the secular, faith and reason, God and the world, church and society, ethics and eschatology. Others besides Pannenberg have been involved. But he has seen the wider, systematic implications more clearly.

His work on *Jesus—God and Man* is of startling originality—firstly in making biblical teaching about Jesus Christ look more credible than it has seemed for many centuries; and secondly in placing very novel interpretations upon these ancient traditions.

Ever since the first generation of Christians, the problem of interpreting the teaching of Jesus about the coming Kingdom of God has been the central problem of Christian theology. We occasionally lose sight of this. Every great theologian has always recalled us to it, and Pannenberg has done this in a very bold manner. It must be admitted that some of his ideas—such as that of the 'ontological priority of the future'—are still in an under-developed condition; but Pannenberg is still a relatively young man. He still has a lot to write. He is currently engaged in working out the basic theory of knowledge underlying his system. We shall hear much more of him in the future.

Chapter 1

THEOLOGICAL ANTHROPOLOGY

THE QUESTION OF GOD AS A HUMAN QUESTION

In 1961 Wolfhart Pannenberg edited and contributed two key essays to *Revelation as History*. This projected a new approach to theology through history. It initiated the programme of subsequent work in what has come to be known as the 'Pannenberg circle'. It might seem best to begin there. I think it better, however, to start with his *What is Man?* The German edition was published a year later than *Revelation as History*. It gives a better impression of Pannenberg's general approach to theology. One might characterize this as an approach 'from below' (borrowing the phrase from his big work of christology, *Jesus—God and Man*).

Like every modern theologian, Pannenberg is faced with the fact that we can no longer presuppose that the term 'God' is understood. We can no longer do theology 'from above', as it were. We must come at it from below.

Something is lost to us. We need to re-traverse the route by which men first came to talk of God. For this reason anthropology has, for our generation, become a necessary element in our approach to metaphysics. In *What is Man?* Pannenberg develops the question of God out of a mainly anthropological study.

In Greek philosophy man was thought of as microcosm—as a reflection of the cosmic structure. Today man understands himself as learning to control the cosmos. He makes models of it

13

only as instruments of his science and technology. He discards these models in favour of others when they no longer serve his purpose. But man's success in thus elevating himself out of nature raises all the more acutely the question: Who or what is man?

Man is distinguished from the rest of nature in the first instance by his 'openness to the world'.[1] An animal has only an environment. Only man has a world. This difference has a biological basis in man's developed senses and nervous system. He perceives in a richer, more complex, more organized way. But that is not the whole difference. Perceiving environment as *world* is a cultural as well as a biological achievement. A human child *learns* to perceive the world. He acquires the world-view of the culture to which he belongs.

At first a child understands himself only from the standpoint of this structured world which he has learned to perceive. He remains, as it were, the prisoner of this world view. Some modern anthropologists will not allow that man ever advances beyond this stage. But this is not what Pannenberg means by 'openness to the world'. If this were all there were to it, then the difference between man and animal would only be one of degree.

True openness to the world consists in the fact that man can always see *beyond* any experience, beyond any particular world-view to new possibilities. He can long for, hope for and strive for such radical novelty.

This is where Pannenberg finds the Greek view of man as the microcosm of a *given* order inadequate.

The excess of motivation which drives man beyond any given world and beyond any particular environment is characteristically human. It expresses itself in play, in taking risks, in laughter. It gives man distance from his world.

This irrepressible restlessness is one of the roots of religion.

---

[1] It is difficult to know how best to translate *Weltoffenheit* as it is used by Pannenberg. It is often translated 'openness to the world'; but it also carries the meaning of having a world which is not self-enclosed but is open towards the contingent, the novel and the transcendent. It thus carries also the sense of openness *beyond* the world.

We cannot, however, say that it is the whole basis or origin of religion. That lies outside man and outside the world in the regions to which hope and longing are directed.

Motivation is always directed towards an object. It expresses itself in effort directed towards food, farm, house, etc. On the animal level nature delimits the needs and environment delimits the objects towards which motivation is directed. But when man, in his openness to the world, breaks these limits he does not simply create fantasies corresponding to his inordinate motives. Rather, the thought of a being transcending the world and standing over against him is already presupposed in the need which he experiences. 'God' is, in the first instance, that toward which man's limitless restlessness is directed. This yields the bare notion of the 'unknown God'. It does not prove his existence.

The whole history of religion is the history of man's relation to this reality which is the counterpart of his infinite restlessness. But in the non-biblical religions 'God' usually remains bound to natural processes, to a cosmic structure, or to a cosmic destiny. Thus the relation to God yields only a partial openness to the world. The modern anthropology of openness to the world has its roots in biblical religion. There God is conceived as wholly transcendent over the world, wholly free in relation to it. So man, conceived in the image of God, is free in relation to the world, is master of it and creative within it. He is also open to possibilities which lie beyond the world. It is because man, in distinction from the beasts, has an open world that the question of God arises for him. The given world can never satisfy him.

Perhaps that means that he should turn away from it in asceticism. In a sense this is true. In order to establish his uniquely free and open relation to the world man has to distance himself from it. But turning away from the world may be either a positive or a negative act. If negative it is mere cynicism. If positive it is done in hope. It is directed expectantly towards what is beyond the world. But the freedom *from* the world which is thus established, is immediately experienced as power *over* the world, and so as responsibility *for* the world.

This is the aspect of human existence which, in biblical tradition, is conceived as man's being 'made in the image of God'. He not only aspires to but somehow also is representative, within creation, of that which infinitely transcends the world. That we experience this more in misery than in fulfilment is beyond dispute. This fact corresponds to the biblical assertion that man has fallen away from his divine image. It is this area of our lives—this infinite aspiration which somehow misses the mark—that we must explore in order to gain a fresher and more lively understanding of the *question* of God.

One thing must be made clear. Pannenberg is emphatic in the view that the question of God—the basic question of theology—is not the special concern of the 'religious' or those who happen to like that sort of thing. It arises out of the structure of human existence and is thus the most fundamental and universal concern of all mankind. Theology, therefore, is as public a discipline as philosophy or natural science. It belongs, in the first instance, in the unversity rather than the seminary.

DOMINION OVER THE WORLD

How does man achieve his unique status of openness toward, freedom from and dominion over the world? In answering this question, we are driven at every level of investigation to refer to his relation to 'that which infinitely transcends the world'.

Imagination is the faculty which enables a man to respond to what is not immediately present in his environment. It is his window on the possibilities which lie beyond immediate actuality.

Allied to the conceptual and organizing power of language, imagination has in man a key role which supersedes that of instinct in animals. It is a mysterious power which we are far from understanding.

It enables us to 'enter into' another man's thoughts, and so understand language in a deeper way. It enables us to recall the past and, even more remarkably, to anticipate the future. Through

16

imagination a man creates and re-creates a world out of his environment. But he not only creates in imagination. He also receives. We speak of radically new ideas as 'coming to us', 'occurring to us', 'striking us' and so on. Imagination is the front on which we are open to the radically new and so to the infinite 'beyond' of the world.

In this perspective God's act of creation is not something that happened distantly once upon a time. It confronts and bears upon us in daily experience.

'The creative nature of imagination has been misunderstood until recently. Characteristically, the Greeks did not distinguish between imagination and memory. They lacked an eye for what is creative, for what is ever new—in the world as well as in man. Only under the influence of the biblical knowledge of God's almighty acts in history was man's view set free for what is creative and new. The creativeness of imagination corresponds to what is new and unforeseeable in external events. But that God constantly produces new things in man's contemplative nature as well as in external history, and that precisely in his creativity man is at the same time completely a recipient, remained concealed for a long time in Western thought.

That man is the creator of his world has become a general conviction in modern times. The question is *how* he produces the artificial world of his language and culture. German idealism regarded man's dominion over the world as based on the power of logical reason. In that way idealism closed itself off from the accidental character of events and from the openness of the future. In the nineteenth century, however, there were also the beginnings of an anthropology that attributed to imagination the leading role in human behaviour.[2] If this is consistently thought through, it results in an understanding of human creativity that not only takes into account the

---

[2] He has in mind Kant's treatment of imagination and its subsequent development through the Romantic Movement.

accidental character of events, but also recognizes the humble reception of inspirations as the source of man's creative power. Thus God appears not only as the goal of man's striving in his openness to the world, but also as the origin of man's creative mastery over the world.' [3]

This is a very attractive suggestion. It has remained a dominant factor in Pannenberg's whole approach to the problems of theology. It places our relationship to God at the centre of all human endeavour rather than confining it to a special religious preserve. It is surely right in seeking the categories in which to interpret the living creator God within our own experience of creativity. It allows history as well as nature to inform our metaphysics.

But at the same time it presents many difficulties. Granted that our most creative ideas seem to come to us 'out of the blue', how can one so readily identify their origin as God? Why not a demon or some departed spirit, as would seem credible in many cultures? Why not a drug or some form of auto-intoxication, as often seems credible in ours?

Even more difficult is the notion of God acting upon our minds. The thought of God by his own agency bringing about particular events in outward history presents difficulty enough. What, for instance, is the nature of the causal relation between God and the event in question? How is this special causality (if causality is the right word) related to day-to-day causality as it operates within the world? But the thought of God bringing about effects within the mind of a person who remains in some respect passive in relation to his activity increases the difficulties. It is clear that Pannenberg does not intend to suggest any kind of divine assault on the integrity of our minds. But it is not entirely clear how all these difficulties are to be avoided or overcome.

It is clear, however, that the main lines of his solution would have much in common with Kant's insistence that the category

[3] Pannenberg, *What is Man?*, pp. 26 ff.

of causality as derived from our understanding of the natural world cannot as such be applied within our experience of free decision. The rational exercise of free creativity in relation to the world and God must be allowed to evolve its own categories. Among such categories are those of 'centredness' and 'openness'. Of these some account will be given shortly (p. 23 below).

In the passage quoted above, Pannenberg is still exploring the idea of God through an examination of man's real relation to what transcends his given world. He is not taking any conventional concept of God for granted. He has already accepted the purely formal characterization of God as that to which man's infinite aspirations are directed. He now offers the suggestion that this object of man's highest aspiration is also the source of his deepest inspiration. It belongs to his essential humanity to stand in such a relation to such a transcendent being. There seems to be good reason both in the history of religion and in the intention of the concept to interpret the idea of God in terms of the essential relationship of our humanity to what lies beyond the immediate actuality of the world.

Man's creative mastery over the world arises from his powers of imagination and invention. The fact that this endless creativity seems to come from beyond himself and from beyond the potential of the given world raises the question of an actively creative God.

TRUST

But mastery over the world is only one aspect of man's openness towards it. No man is ever completely in charge of his situation. Therefore openness to the world calls for trust as well as mastery. Trust is basically letting oneself go. But a man can let himself go only in the expectation that there is something he can depend on. Placing one's trust in people and things is part of everyday living. But these particular acts of trust arise out of an ultimate trust. In this respect Luther was right in saying that God and faith belong together. To live his life a man has to be able to let himself go. In so doing he trusts. In trusting he acknowledges God, whether he realizes this or not.

Naturally, one prefers not to take things on trust wherever one can establish mastery over them. That is what technology is all about. But there are some relationships which are destroyed by this. Personal relationships are destroyed when we try to substitute mastery for trust. Most of all our relation to God is destroyed by such a substitution.

Mastery is the proper human relationship to things. This is the relationship we strive to achieve. Trust is the proper relationship to God, and to our fellow men who share that relationship with us.

These two elements of mastery and trust are not independent of one another. In order to achieve mastery over the world, our imagination and our longing must be directed towards what infinitely transcends the world—and so to God.

But when men seek a short-cut to security these relationships reverse roles. Trust is placed in the finite objects of the world and mastery of the infinite is sought.

This happens in religion when the infinite is made available within the finite in idol and cult. Pannenberg suggests that idolatry is really the beginning of the process which ends in that total secularization of the world which is a prominent feature of modern technological civilization. Once the object of man's infinite aspiration is encapsulated within the world—in the processes of nature and in the symbols of the cult—then it is but one more step to the realization that the gods amount to nothing—that one can deal directly with the finite world as world and learn to master it by technical control.[4]

But this means that man's capacity for infinite aspiration can

---

[4] This runs counter to the interpretation of the history of religion in much modern theology. Barth identifies 'religion' with this kind of cultic worship. He distinguishes biblical *faith* in the wholly transcendent and sovereign God sharply from 'religion'. This faith is therefore the end of 'religion'. Dietrich Bonhoeffer developed this line of thought in his concept of 'secular Christianity'. In America the 'death of God' theologians took it to what appeared to be its logical conclusion.

be directed only toward the world. He must entrust himself wholly to it. He is forced to attempt to make the relation of trust coincide with that of mastery. But these relationships are incompatible. Thus man, through his trust becomes enslaved to the object of his mastery. Through his mastery he becomes alienated from the object of his trust.[5] This is how man experiences that depravity which is symbolized in the myth of the Fall. Modern man experiences this as bondage to the creations of his own technology, and as alienation within its structures, whether capitalist or communist.

That freedom from the world, which is the basis of true mastery over it, can be achieved only on the basis of a trust directed to what infinitely transcends the world. This occurred for the first time, Pannenberg thinks, in the Judaeo-Christian revelation. It is certainly significant that those cultures which have attained a high degree of scientific and technical mastery over the world have historical roots in the Judaeo-Christian tradition.[6]

Thus the dialectic of mastery and trust in our dealing with the world raises the question of God.

HOPE

Openness to what transcends the world has a very marked effect on man's relation to his own future. He can foresee it in imagination, bring it about in mastery, fear it in mistrust, hope for it in trust. All other creatures live wholly in the present. Man's interest is always directed into the future. He arranges and provides for his future. But there is a limit to what he can do in that respect.

---

[5] On this point Pannenberg might well have made fuller use of Hegel's profound analysis of the lord–slave relation in *The Phenomenology of Mind* (tr. J. B. Baillie, Allen & Unwin, 1931, pp. 228–40).

[6] Put without qualification, this is perhaps a rather cavalier historical judgment. One wonders, for example, why the people of Israel were themselves so singularly barren of scientific achievement. A good case can be made out for the view that the biblical revelation had something to do with the rise of Western science and technology. But Greek rationality and Arab ingenuity also played their part.

The future always contains an element that is essentially unpredictable and uncontrollable. Hope begins where management ends. Yet it is hope that inspires the effort to manage the world.

In the perspective of hope the future is an open field for imagination. Present hope pictures future fulfilment. This is the basis on which Pannenberg is able to elevate the apocalyptic tradition from the status of a purely Jewish phenomenon to one of universal human relevance. Man's openness to what infinitely transcends his immediate environment drives him to commit himself to the open future either in the hope of unlimited fulfilment or in fretful anxiety. The outstanding feature of the religion of Israel is the stress which it places—really for the first time in the history of religions—on both the novelty and the reliability of the future as something to be hoped for. This is what the faithfulness of God meant to the people of Israel. This is the basis of the theology of promise and fulfilment.

The question whether hope is wisdom or madness rests ultimately on the question whether there is anything to hope for beyond death. Man alone can foresee his death and appreciate its threat to hope's fulfilment. Death thus foreseen makes nonsense of hope. But it does not allow us to retreat from hope into the simple enjoyment of the present. It makes all present enjoyment shallow. Only the man who can have confidence and hope in his future is able to abandon himself to living the present moment. To let hope reach out beyond death is as natural to man as to foresee his death.

Pannenberg lays great stress on the distinction between two forms of this hope. One finds typical expression in Greek thought. The Greeks hoped for the continued life of the soul after death in separation from the body. Being intellectual it is not subject to corruption and change. It is therefore, they believed, imperishable. The other view finds its typical expression in the Hebrew tradition. The Hebrews stressed the indissoluble unity of body and soul and admitted the absolute seriousness of death as the end of life. But they also learned to hope for resurrection as a new, creative act of God. This reached its highest development and expression in the apocalyptic tradition.[7]

In Pannenberg's opinion the belief that the immaterial soul has a natural immortality is no longer a viable option. Modern biology and psychology, he believes, have established so intimate a connection between body and soul that that possibility is no longer thinkable. I confess I do not find this conclusion quite so self-evident. But certainly, if the soul has no natural immortality, then hope too raises the question of God as the one who raises up the dead.

OPENNESS AND CENTREDNESS

Man's unique openness to and beyond the world is balanced by a high degree of centredness. Every organism lives by balancing openness and exclusiveness. Even a plant not only ingests nourishment from its environment. It also maintains its structure against the inroads of its environment. This tension is more acute in animals. It is of problematic intensity in man, for man is at once the most open and the most highly centred of all creatures. He cannot depend upon his biological structure and his instincts to keep his person intact. In the face of the openness and contingency of his future—of all that comes to meet him on the way—he must actively select not only his nourishment but his destiny. He selects his destiny out of the occasions and opportunities made available to him. In so doing he discovers who he is. Maintaining the integrity and centredness of his own person is deliberate as well as instinctual. Yet his unique openness makes this all the more vulnerable.

Men may respond to this tension in either of two ways. Which-

---

[7] This account of the contrast between the Greek and Hebrew traditions is broadly true. But it involves some rather sweeping generalizations. Pannenberg frequently uses the Hebrews and the Greeks as representative types rather than with reference to the complex variety of their cultural traditions. This is legitimate for some illustrative purposes, but it is a little surprising in one who, as we shall see, sets so much store by strictly historical method.

ever way they respond, it remains a basic dilemma of human existence.

Firstly, a man, giving strong expression to the centredness of his person, may assert himself against his environment. He may do so both defensively and aggressively. If he does so aggressively he becomes the sort of person who feels a compulsion to establish himself as master in every situation. He is prepared to subject the whole world to his own self-centredness. He cannot afford to acknowledge the centred integrity of anyone or anything else. This is the relation to the world which in medieval times was called concupiscence. (Originally that word did not have the narrowly sexual connotation it now has.) In its most extreme development it becomes delusional insanity. It is the way of the paranoid. The subject tries to preserve the centredness of the self by including everything within its circle.

If an exaggerated expression of centredness takes a defensive form it operates by exclusion. The centre of the self is defended by keeping the circle closed so as to exclude the world—to exclude everything that is not self. This is the way of the ascetic. It is withdrawal into the self in narcissistic purity. In its most extreme development this is the way of the depressive. In suppressing openness to the world it impairs the capacity for response.

But secondly, a man may one-sidedly deny his centredness in the name of openness. He is active and open to every stimulus, but has no policy. He is outer-directed. He loses himself in whatever happens to be going on. The self-centred man seeks by a kind of spiritual heroism to be master. The man who abandons himself in openness accepts slavery.

Pannenberg tends to emphasize exaggerated self-centredness as an expression of sin. He is inclined to neglect the possibility that sin may equally come to expression in the opposite way by sheer self-abandonment. The fundamental problem of human existence is not simply that of overcoming self-centredness. It is to find a relationship in which the tension between self-

24

centredness and openness is overcome without the destruction of either.

The tension between centredness and openness is a tension between self and world. It is inherent in the subject–object structure of human consciousness. It cannot therefore be resolved within the structure of man's inner-worldly experience but can be resolved only by reference to a transcendent common ground of both self and world. Thus the tension between centredness and openness raises the question of God.

It is clear that the background to Pannenberg's analysis of the tension between centredness and openness is Hegel's account of 'unhappy consciousness' in *The Phenomenology of Mind* as the alienation of the conscious subject from the world as the object of consciousness. He also follows Hegel in showing that this operates at a social and cultural level as well as at the individual and personal level. It takes the form of a tension between the free self-determination of each centred self and the demands of society. Thus in its social context the tension between centredness and openness gives rise to alienation. The centred self resists alien influence. It resists and resents the intrusion of society and of every reality outside itself upon it. It wishes to master reality as the realm of its own self-expression. Yet the self is dependent upon society and upon the world. Therefore it has to recognize this external reality which is strange to it. In recognizing and submitting to such external authority the centred self becomes enslaved. Man is thus alienated from himself as well as from society. There is thus a social dialectic of centredness and openness as well as a private and personal one.

The intimate relation between Hegel and Pannenberg is of more than merely historical or academic interest. As we shall see, it is by no means always one of agreement. But there are always points of contact.

No theology which fails to relate consciously, in sympathy and in tension, to Hegel can be socially and culturally relevant in the modern world. Whatever may be the fate of Hegelian idealism as a system of philosophy, concepts deriving ultimately from Hegel form the root-stock of sociology. This came about through the work of Feuerbach and Marx who together turned theology into sociology. It now seems clear that theology cannot fight back effectively with mere counter-suggestions. The counter-attack can be effective only by showing that sociology leads back to theology. In the last analysis it raises theological questions.

Hegel saw the problem of alienation in society as an extension of the problem of what Pannenberg calls centredness and openness. He looked for a solution in the development of absolute Spirit or Reason. This he identified with the God of the Christian tradition. But he saw the whole story of creation, the election of Israel, incarnation, resurrection and final triumph of the kingdom as symbolic of a process immanent within man. God actualizes himself within human society and culture. This, at least, is what Hegel was taken to mean.

Feuerbach made the next move. A God who is not wholly identified with man is a symbol of man's alienation from his true self and from society. The proper object of man's ultimate trust, love and aspiration is the human species itself. This is his true God.

Marx followed Feuerbach. He made the analysis more concrete. He expressed it in economic terms. It is private ownership of the means of production that creates the master–slave relation. Remove that factor from the situation and alienation is overcome. There is then no more need for religion.

This development from Hegel to Marx and its further outworking in modern sociology is the most momentous thing that has happened to theology since the Reformation. In the main theologians have tried to continue as though it had never happened. Pannenberg, however, is compellingly aware that it did.

He traces the fundamental error back to Hegel himself. He uses a good deal of Hegel's method and defends much in his philosophy. But he lays two serious faults at Hegel's door. Firstly, he did not fully recognize the finitude of human reason. Secondly, he left no room for an element of genuine contingency in human affairs. It was because of the first error that he made the mistake of identifying the divine action of revelation and reconciliation directly and unambiguously with the self-development of human reason in history. It was only because of the second error that he was able to treat world history as a self-enclosed process including the transcendent within itself. It was these errors in Hegel that opened the way for Feuerbach and Marx along their mistaken path.

Avoid these Hegelian errors. Make full use of the vast areas of truth in Hegel's philosophy. Then Pannenberg suggests you will see that the problem of alienation—the problem of a contradictory relation between the individual and society—raises the question of a ground of reconciliation which transcends both. It raises the question of God.[8]

TIME AND ETERNITY

The tension between centredness and openness affects every aspect of life. The objects of the world are accessible to us only as we open ourselves to them. We do so in acknowledging their objective existence as independent of ourselves. The centre of their existence is in themselves, not in us. This is true of things as well as people.

Yet, on the other hand, we see everything from our own point of view. We see things in relation to ourselves and our own interest. We experience them in terms of our own ideas and images and our own forms of perception. This is the self-centred aspect of experience.

If we assert the centred structure of our existence in total opposition to openness, then we close ourselves against reality. This is the essence of sin. We close ourselves off from the world

[8] In taking this line Pannenberg is met half-way by sociologists such as Peter Berger who is prepared to say, 'What could be in the making here is a gigantic joke on Feuerbach.' (*A Rumour of Angels*, Allen Lane, 1971, p. 64.) The theory that God is only a projection of the human spirit in alienation and the whole philosophy built upon it may itself be an illusory projection of the human spirit. 'What appears as a human projection in one may appear as a reflection of divine realities in another.' (*Ibid.*, p. 64.)

and from God. Nothing can have reality or significance except in relation to ourselves.

In his experience of space, and even more in his experience of time, the self-centred man is enclosed within himself, shut away from God and from the reality of the world. But such self-enclosure is never complete. Even the sinner is nourished in spirit as well as in body from God's world. Man can never completely repress that openness which is an essential feature of his humanity.

Each of us experiences space as centred upon himself. What is 'up' to one man is 'down' to another. What is 'here' to one man is 'there' to another. The space which a man experiences is centred upon his own presence. Similarly with time. The time which he experiences is centred upon his own present. Both space and time, as they are experienced by finite beings, are relative to the standpoint of the observer. What is future to me now will one day be someone's present. What is past to me now was once someone's future.

What is the truth about space and time? Does it lie in my perspective or the other man's? If I insist on the reality of myself as a centred being, then I must take my viewpoint as valid, my space as real, my time as real. But if in humility and openness I acknowledge the reality of other people and other things not merely in their relation to me but as centred in themselves, then I must acknowledge the validity of their viewpoint on space and time.

There is a difficulty and a contradiction here. One solution would be to find an absolute point of reference, independent of all observers, within space and time. Mythological space and time are usually credited with such a point of reference. Space centres upon the supporting pillar of the world, or upon the Holy City, or upon some prominent astronomical feature such as the sun. Time centres upon the archetypal events which set the pattern for the world's subsequent happening, upon the birth and death of gods, upon the golden age, and so on.

Such myths have lost credibility in the face of both science and the prophetic criticism in the Judaeo-Christian tradition. But from that tradition there has come also an alternative suggestion —that the absolute point of reference lies outside both space and time. The absolute point of reference lies neither in my past, my present nor my future, but in the God who transcends space and time as we know them. It is only for creatures embedded within time that time falls apart into a past which is no more and a future which is not yet. From a standpoint outside time as we know it the order of events would remain (for time is irreversible) but they would be gathered together in a total compresence.

This is a concept so important for Pannenberg's doctrine of God that it is essential to grasp it as clearly as possible. In particular, there are two facile responses to this suggestion that must be avoided. The first is to say 'Eternity outside time! We know about that. The Greeks were onto it a long time ago.' This is not at all what Pannenberg has in mind. We shall deal with the contrast between Pannenberg's view of eternity and the Greek (Platonic) view in connection with the doctrine of God (below, pp. 93–8). It will suffice for the moment to say that in the Greek—specifically the Platonic—view of eternity, it consists in dissociation from change and becoming in time. In Pannenberg's view, the eternity of God consists precisely in the universal intimacy of his relation to all time and to all process.

The second temptation is to treat his views on the relation of time and eternity as arbitrary metaphysical speculation without empirical foundation. This is a singularly inappropriate criticism of a man who, as we shall see, is far more deeply imbued with the spirit of history than metaphysics. His elucidation of the concept of eternity as the compresence of all times to God has an empirical basis. It is explained in relation to the phenomenology of our experience of time.

From an external point of view, the present is simply a dividing line between past and future. In itself it has no duration. But in fact we experience the present as having duration. It is as though our present were a standing wave in the river of time.

Like our horizon, it travels with us wherever we go. Or, to change the metaphor, our present bridges time.

The duration of the experienced 'present' may vary according to circumstance and context. In politics the 'present' situation may last for months. In a car accident the present may shrink to a fraction of a second.

The span of our present depends largely on the degree of our control over the situation as well as upon the speed of events. An event belongs to our present so long as we can still make decisions about it determining its course. Whatever has passed beyond our sphere of influence belongs to the past. Whatever has not yet evoked our response belongs to the future. This means that past events, in so far as they still concern us also have a foothold in the present.

Our present is that span of the world's happening about which we can still do something and so is on our agenda. It is a function of what we know and what we can do.

Our own experience of an extended present enables us to give meaning to the notion of an infinitely extended present. It involves the concept of one who, unlike us, does not experience time and space as a limitation but is omniscient and omnipotent. These attributes are the conditions of omnipresence in space and time.

Thus our experience of time raises the question of God. In this respect, Pannenberg suggests, modern theory of space–time relativity goes hand in hand with faith. Together they express man's wholesome desire to let reality be what it is in itself, instead of understanding it only in relation to his own self-centredness.

In spiritual, scientific, political and economic life—even in personal relations and private conversation—we are attempting to establish a shared, common world. It is only thus that alienation can be overcome and true community established. So we have to raise the question of a truth which is valid for everyone.

'The truth of time lies beyond the self-centredness of our experience of time as past, present, and future. The truth of time is the occurrence of all events in an eternal present. Eternity, then, does not stand in contrast to time as something that is completely different. Eternity creates no other content than time. However, eternity is the truth of time, which remains hidden in the flux of time. Eternity is the unity of all time, but as such it simultaneously is something that exceeds our experience of time. The perception of all events in an eternal present would be possible only from a point beyond the stream of time. Such a position is not attainable for any finite creature. Only God can be thought of as not being confined to the flow of time. Therefore, eternity is God's time. That means, however, that God is present to every time. His action and power extend to everything past and future as to something that, for him, is present.' [9]

This is the basis of the unity of the world. Without that there is no possibility of unity in society. It is only in this way that man can experience himself as belonging to a world rather than the world as belonging to him.

MAN—THE HISTORICAL ANIMAL: GOD—THE GOD OF HISTORY

But all these approaches to man—the anthropological, the sociological, the political and so on—miss the concreteness of man. Aristotle described man as a rational animal. But that abstracts only one aspect of him. Only history exhibits man in all his concreteness. Therefore it is the question of the meaning of history that raises the puestion of God in the most concrete and pressing way.

The view that it is his historicity which distinguishes man from every other creature has been frequently put forward in modern times, e.g. by Bultmann, Gogarten, H. R. Niebuhr, R. Gregor Smith. But for the most part it is the bare, essential structure of historicity rather than concrete history that they have in mind. It is not concrete history as it is investigated and interpreted by historians. By 'history' Pannenberg does not mean 'historicity'. He means history as it actually happened. Yet in some respects he means something narrower than that. By 'history' he means events which are consciously experienced and recorded as history. In human perspective what happens in nature without a consciously recognized relation to man does not belong to history. But, from the divine perspective, as part of God's history, it belongs to the whole of history.

So long as man felt himself immersed in nature he could not experience his human existence in all its distinctiveness as history. He lacked that openness beyond the world and the contrasting intensive centredness which form the warp and woof of history. So long as man's gods were immersed in nature he could not achieve this openness. Time was conceived as cyclical within a natural frame of reference. The model for understanding human events in time was the wheeling of the stars and the rotation of the seasons.[10]

It was in the history of Israel that history, in what Pannenberg takes to be the true and proper sense, was for the first time experienced as such. This was because it was experienced as the self-disclosure of a God who, unlike the Canaanite *baalim*, was not bound to nature. He transcended the world absolutely. In relation to this revelation and by virtue of it, man attained true openness beyond the world. So he became, in the sense intended by Pannenberg, a historical being.

In our understanding of history in the modern world we are the heirs of that tradition. We need to re-discover our own inheritance.

When we say that man is an essentially historical being this means more than that he determines his own destiny through free decision. Existentialist analyses of the human situation exaggerate the importance of decision (and so of free self-centredness). Man also receives his history in what befalls him.

[10] Cf. M. Eliade, *The Myth of the Eternal Return* (Routledge & Kegan Paul, 1954).

As a man opens himself to the world, the chain of events which make up his history form the pattern of his individuality. But on the other hand, this is not something that happens by nature. A man must actively seek his destiny. In this, consciously or unconsciously, he is seeking God. He is seeking fulfilment in the eternity of God. Where this quest is conscious, the free decision of the centred self is seen as response to the leading of God. What befalls him is experienced as sent by God.

Historical life is life lived in search of the meaning of what befalls us. But the life of an individual man cannot have meaning in itself. It can have meaning only in relation to a significant whole. Such a significant whole cannot be taken for granted. History does not have a natural unity in itself. It divides into periods, nations and cultures separated in space and time. Only a being who spans the whole of space and time in his knowledge and action can constitute the unity of history and determine the meaning of the whole.

In this way historical existence raises the question of God.

The Israelites were the first to see that what the future will contain cannot be worked out or determined beforehand. The future is not the outworking of previous events (as a characteristic theme of Greek tragedy tends to suggest). They saw the contingency and novelty of each new thing that came upon them as the creative activity of God. They thought of God as wholly free in relation to the world, yet ceaselessly active within it. Nothing can happen except by his activity. 'Shall evil befall a city and the Lord hath not done it?' (Amos 3:6).

Their understanding of history was inseparable from their theology. In inheriting this understanding of history, the modern world has increasingly treated the theology as an irrelevance. But without the theology the truth of history—the truth about its meaning—loses its stable point of reference and breaks up into relativity. Its unity disintegrates under the pressure of the centredness of the individual structures within it. It is no longer possible for us to write universal history.

Israel's experience of reality as historical rested on the belief

33

that the world is created and sustained by God. It rested on the belief that it is by his action that events come upon us out of the future. It rested on the belief that all times and places are bound together in their compresence to God. It rested on the belief that the meaning of our history is determined by the fact that it is our history *with* God. It rested on the belief that God gave and fulfilled his promises in history. It rested on the belief that God disclosed himself in the events of history.

Chapter 2

REVELATION AS HISTORY

The idea that Revelation is a historical event rather than a set of divinely authorized doctrines is not peculiar to Pannenberg. But he has upheld this idea with a thorough-going emphasis peculiarly his own. It is the key concept of his theology.

REVELATION AS DOCTRINE

The word 'revelation' has come to play an exaggerated role in modern theology. This is largely because of the difficulties and embarrassments to which it has given rise. In the period of Protestant Orthodoxy in the seventeenth century an exaggerated emphasis was placed on the verbal and propositional aspect of revelation.

There is nothing illogical or irrational in accepting a statement on authority. We do it in all walks of life every day. For example, having every reason to believe that a doctor is competent and qualified, we accept his diagnosis as authoritative. There are known test-procedures to establish the competence of such an authority.

It is altogether another matter when we come upon an absolute claim to authority—a claim to untested and untestable authority —such as is not uncommon in religion. In the name of revelation this was the claim that was made for biblical and doctrinal statements in the seventeenth century.

In this sense the appeal to the absolute authority of

'revealed' statements is an affront to responsible rationality. In that flowering of autonomous reason known as the Enlightenment, in the eighteenth century, this crude view of dogmatic authority came under heavy criticism. The spirit of the eighteenth century is typified in the title of Kant's *Religion Within the Limits of Reason Alone*. Revelation conceived as a body of divinely communicated, unquestionable, infallible truths was attacked from every side—by science, by philosophy, and perhaps most of all by the new science of history. Immanuel Kant wrote in 1798:

> 'The biblical theologian shows that God exists because he has spoken in the Bible ... But it is neither possible nor legitimate for the biblical theologian as such to establish that God himself has in fact spoken through the Bible. That is a question of history.'[1]

This view of revelation never really survived the criticisms of the Enlightenment. It survives only in the intellectual ghettos of modern fundamentalism (Catholic or Protestant).

One of the refreshing and attractive features of Wolfhart Pannenberg is the intellectual zest with which he greets the critical rationality of the Enlightenment. He asks no special favours for theology and makes an ally out of what appeared to be the most insidious enemy of all—critical history.

But before coming to Pannenberg we must take brief note of the developments that led up to his concept of revelation as history.

In response to the discrediting of the conception of revelation as a body of divinely sanctioned truths two important moves were made in the nineteenth century.

REVELATION AS THE SELF-DISCLOSURE OF GOD

On the one hand Schleiermacher identified revelation with the

[1] *Der Streit der Fakultäten*, volume 9 of *Werke*, ed. Wilhelm Weischedel, p. 285.

self-disclosure of God in religious experience. But this tended—
and still tends—to evaporate into various forms of subjectivism.

On the other hand Hegel conceived of revelation as the self-
disclosure of the Absolute. In a very different form—but with
affinities to Hegel which Pannenberg stresses more than most
interpreters—Karl Barth has taken up this notion of revelation
as the self-disclosure of God.

Pannenberg acknowledges this history and takes up the problem at this point. He retains a profound respect for Schleiermacher
—especially his work in laying the foundations of modern
theological hermeneutics—but he rejects his subjective interpretation of revelation. He rejects it on the ground that faith
cannot be generated out of itself. It must be occasioned by an
external event. This is also his reason for rejecting R. Bultmann's
existentialist interpretation of the revealing and saving events
of the New Testament. He regards Bultmann as in the direct
line of succession to Schleiermacher's subjectivism.

Barth's suggestion that revelation is properly to be thought
of as the self-disclosure of God in historic events is more cordially
received. But important reservations are made. For Barth the
primary medium of God's self-disclosure is the 'Word' of God.
Whether Barth means by this the Holy Scriptures, the second
Person in the Trinity or the preached word or all three is not
always clear. In many contexts it does appear to be an authoritative, self-authenticating propositional 'Word' and so is not
wholly free from the criticisms of the Enlightenment.

Some theologians of the post-Bultmann school, such as Fuchs
and Ebeling, have come nearer to a historical understanding of
revelation as the self-disclosure of God in the concept of Word-
event or Speech-event.

REVELATION AS EVENT

Pannenberg proposes a thorough-going, historical interpretation
of revelation as self-disclosure. Revelation *is* historical event.
It is historical event interpreted as 'act of God'.

The origin of this understanding of revelation is found in the religion of Israel. They experienced their own history as the self-disclosure of a God who was faithful to them. He led them across the Red Sea out of Egypt. He led them into the land of Canaan. He led them into battle against their enemies and gave them victory. He led them away captive to purify them with suffering only to come and redeem them again.

But, it may be objected, this does not really take us away from the view of revelation as a set of statements. We must distinguish between the historical events themselves and the *interpretation* which the Israelites placed upon those events. The interpretations amount to a set of doctrines.

Pannenberg meets this objection head-on. He denies that such an absolute distinction between event and interpretation is valid. We can draw it abstractly; but we cannot apply it in practice. The meaning of events inheres in them. (This is crucial to his whole position.) The 'brute facts' of positivist thought are pure abstractions. They do not exist concretely in the world. Facts are always experienced in a context in which they have significance. The analysis which separates a fact from its significance arises only from subsequent reflection.

He is not playing with any kind of medieval Realism at this point. He is not toying with some latter-day version of the reality of the universal concept in the thing it names. His first line of defence appears to be *Gestalt* psychology and epistemology. We perceive significant wholes in the first instance and analyse them into their elements only in special and unfamiliar acts of introspective and logical analysis. But he does not rest his whole case on that. He prefers to argue historically, dealing with a large context rather than the minutiae of perception.

The kind of event that becomes the object of the historian's interest is singled out by him from the continuum of the world's happening because of its apparent significance. It is this significance which constitutes it as a unity standing out from the flow of events. The historian may be mistaken about its significance. He may be mistaken about the kind of fact it is. In order to check or correct his own view of its significance he does not attempt to isolate 'brute fact' from interpretation. He is more likely to cast his search for significance wider. He asks about the motives of the authors of the documentary evidence he is using. He relates the event to what he knows of the cultural context of its own times. He considers the difference between that context and the context of his own times. This alters his perspective and so perhaps causes him to perceive the significance of the event differently. He casts about for a wider frame of reference in which he can bring the two perspectives together in the same field of focus.

There are checking procedures by which we test whether we have rightly seen the significance of an event. But they do not simply consist in isolating the 'brute facts' from all interpretation.

This approach brings Pannenberg's interest in the inherence of significance in events more into the field of historical hermeneutics than that of metaphysics or epistemology.

His view of the relation of fact and meaning in historical event is very close to that of R. G. Collingwood to whom he refers with approval. Collingwood spoke of events as having an 'inside' and an 'outside'. The inside of an event or fact is the meaning it has within its total context for those whose experience it touches.

But meaning in events must surely always be meaning *for somebody*. Pannenberg readily agrees. When he speaks of meanings as inherent in events, he is not suggesting that they have some ghostly existence of their own.

'The natural events that are involved in the history of a people have no meaning apart from the connection with the traditions and expectations in which men live. The events of history speak their own language, the language of facts; however, this language is understandable only in the context of the traditions and the expectations in which the given events occur.' [2]

But the interpretation is part of the event. It is not something

---

[2] Pannenberg, *Revelation as History*, p. 152 f., cf. *Theology as History*, pp. 125 ff.

external to it. The development of the interpretation is part of the event's history and a major factor in its continuity with the rest of the world's happening.

But here we run into a difficulty. The same event may have different meanings for different people. Therefore must we not conclude that the meaning of events is after all something subjective and in no sense inherent in the events themselves? No!— not as long as there are rational and objective methods by which we can dispute and settle the truth-claims of such interpretations. For example, we may correct our view of the significance inherent in an event by reference to the expectations which that description of the event raises. Many people experienced the Second World War as the 'liberation of Europe'. Subsequent events in the continent of Europe may have caused them to revise their interpretation of 'what really happened' in those dreadful struggles. The fact that we acknowledge the legitimacy of such attempts to correct the interpretation of historic events implies that there *is* a correct interpretation at which we aim. In this sense, Pannenberg's conception of meaning as inherent in events is legitimate.

Judgements about the meaning of historic events are always open to review. They are therefore open also to difference of opinion. But difference of opinion does not imply the subjectivity of these opinions. The science of critical history is the known and accredited method of settling such differences with reference to the objective significance of the events concerned. Even where the description of events is traditio-historical material claiming for these events the significance of a divine self-disclosure, the method of verifying such a claim is still that of critical history.[3] The history which purports to be revelatory must be studied in its continuity with the rest of history. Precisely the same methods of investigation and criteria of verification are appliable.

In the light of what we have said, how could the events of the

---

[3] One might have said 'critical history precisely as it is practised by the secular historian'. This essentially is Pannenberg's intention; but put like that it needs to be qualified by the fact that in Pannenberg's view contemporary historians tend to misunderstand their own task, being largely infected by a positivistic philosophy of history.

history of Israel ever be interpreted as the self-disclosure of God? First of all, the truly novel, the contingent, the unforeseeable—which is what distinguishes history from nature—raises the question of the creative source of the new thing that has come into being. Just as radical novelty in the inner life of thought and imagination was found to raise the question of God (above, p. 16 ff.), so also does it in the outward life of history.

One can, of course, evade the question by asserting that every event, no matter how new it appears to be, must be wholly explicable in terms of its antecedent causes—a modern kind of dogmatism! (Dogmatism, whether ecclesiastical or secular, is never the ally of revelation. Dogmatism resists all novelty. Revelation on the other hand, to qualify as revelation, must disclose something that is quite new.)

One can evade the question of God as it arises out of the really new and unforeseeable in history by ascribing such novelty to sheer chance—a modern form of irrationalism! (It is questionable whether absolute randomness is even a thinkable concept.)

But it is surely not altogether unreasonable to consider the possibility that such novelty may be the creative influence of a power transcending the observable world order whose mode of operation is not open to our inspection.

Such a view would, of course, be sheer mythology were it not subject to some sort of test procedure. But, Pannenberg argues, it is open to quite exacting test procedures. For example, the interpretation of the escape from Egypt as an act of the God of Israel raised certain expectations. In so far as subsequent history confirmed these expectations the interpretation was justified. In fact, the subsequent experience of Israel was such that, for those who participated in it, it seemed (*a*) to confirm the faithfulness of Jahweh to his people but also (*b*) to call for constant revision and refinement of their understanding of that faithful relationship.[4]

---

[4] In this he is strongly influenced by Gerhard von Rad's treatment of the theology of the Old Testament and more specifically by the essay 'The Concept of Revelation in Ancient Israel' contributed by Rolf Rendtorff to *Revelation as History*.

The expectations raised by the significant events came to be expressed in the traditions of Israel as the promise of Jahweh. The ever ambiguous confirmation of these expectations came to be known as fulfilment. So the religion of Israel became the religion of promise and fulfilment. But Pannenberg never allows these favourite terms of biblical theology to exercise their familiar mystique. They are never allowed to elope from the control of sober historical judgement into the realm of mythological credulity or gnostic secret knowledge.

Because of this, Pannenberg eventually came to reject the terms 'promise and fulfilment' as misleading and prefers to speak of 'the history of the transmission of tradition'.[5] This takes better account of the way in which an event which is experienced as 'full of promise' is often transformed in its meaning in the course of its outworking in history so that the promise comes to be interpreted through the fulfilment and 'the interpretation can be full of surprises even for the prophet himself'.[6]

One is left with the impression that, for him, the question of whether Israel's interpretation of her own history as the leading of God in promise and fulfilment is to be answered in precisely the same way and by precisely the same methods as would be appropriate to deciding whether the people of the United States of America were historically justified in understanding their own actions in modern history as 'keeping the world safe for democracy', or whether the people of Gaullist France were justified in regarding themselves as the bearers of civilization in the modern world, or the Russian people in regarding themselves as the true representatives of the working classes of the world. I find this very refreshing after the hot-house atmosphere in which most forms of 'revealed' theology seem to thrive.

In this respect Pannenberg contrasts sharply with other modern

[5] Pannenberg, *Basic Questions in Theology*, Vol. I, p. xvii.
[6] Walter Zimmerli, 'Promise and Fulfilment' in C. Westermann (ed.), *Essays on Old Testament Interpretations*, SCM, London, 1963, p. 107. cf. Pannenberg, *Basic Questions in Theology*, Vol. I, p. 27.

theologians who have emphasized the historical character of revelation as the self-disclosure of God. A generation before Pannenberg Barth and Brunner had emphasized the historical particularity of the manifestation of the Word of God as a saving event. But for both of them this redemptive happening is separated off from the rest of history. Its meaning is available only to faith, not to critical history. Barth refers to this—particularly the events of the incarnation—as 'primordial history' (*Urgeschichte*). Pannenberg sees this as an unhistorical, mythological concept, more gnostic than Christian in character.

Bultmann has also stressed the historical particularity of the revealing event as it occurred in Jesus Christ. But he relies heavily on the somewhat artificial distinction (first used in this way by M. Kähler) between what the Germans refer to as *Historie* and *Geschichte*. Very roughly, he takes *Historie* to be the bare recounting of the facts. *Geschichte* is history interpreted in its existential significance for us. The history of saving, revealing events in this latter sense is therefore rightly understood only in the existential decision of faith, not in the judgements of scientific, critical history.

Pannenberg rejects the epistemological dualism of this distinction. It rests, he suggests, on questionable philosophical premises. It accepts too readily the currently prevalent positivistic assumptions about the nature of factual knowledge. It separates fact and interpretation in the manner criticized above. It bears the mark of what is loosely described as 'neo-Kantian dualism'. It divorces the actual content of the revealing events—the actual history of Israel and the life of Jesus—from their significance as bare disclosure of the existential structure of authentic human existence.

For Bultmann the results of historical research into the life of Jesus, whether positive or negative, are of no ultimate theological significance. He divorces the 'that' from the 'what' of history. He reduces the concrete history of the saving events to the bare form of their historicity. This is ultimately an escape from history. It is an escape from the concreteness of history into the realm of timeless 'gnostic' truths open to the existentially initiate but closed to others.

In some respects Oscar Cullmann comes nearest to anticipating Pannenberg's thorough-going historicism. But his concept of *Heilsgeschichte* or 'salvation history' is in the last analysis mythological and ahistorical. It separates off a special strand of history consisting of Israel, Jesus and the church from the rest of history. This special, saving history has to be approached with special attitudes and assumptions. One has to 'align' oneself with it in faith in order to see its meaning. One rejects this meaning under pain of divine judgement.

In criticism of Karl Löwith's dependence on Cullmann, Pannenberg says: 'He does not understand that redemptive history is not supra-history, but because of its universal tendency essentially includes all events.'[7] He goes on to say: 'A general collapse of historical method must result if there exists alongside it another, more fruitful way to certainty about past events.'[8]

If revelatory events have meaning in the same sense as any other historical event, some acute questions arise. Does this mean that theologians should simply become historians? There is a sense in which Pannenberg does tend to turn his historians into theologians and his theologians into historians.

According to him, the method and interest of the historian and the theologian are essentially the same. The only difference is that the historian is typically interested in interpreting the facts in relation to a specific, limited area or period. The theologian, on the other hand, is interested in the self-disclosure of the universal God in history. He is concerned with specific events and periods only in so far as they illuminate the meaning of history as a whole.

Universal history is not a popular concept with professional historians. They see it more as an area of speculation than of firm, historical research. But against this Pannenberg maintains

[7] *Basic Questions*, Vol. I, p. 32.
[8] *Ibid.* p., 38.

that every judgement by a historian about the significance of events is made on the basis of some assumptions, however rudimentary and vague, about what human history as a whole is all about. This is the sense in which every historian is, in Pannenberg's view, a kind of crypto-theologian.

Chapter 3

FAITH AND HISTORY

This close association of history and theology raises the question of the relation of critical history to faith in a particularly acute form. This is a problem which has always existed for the Judaeo-Christian tradition. It has, however, become particularly acute since the rise of critical history in the Enlightenment. Historical judgements are at best probable. Faith is an attitude of unwavering belief and total trust. How, then, can faith be founded upon historical judgements?

Since the failure of all the attempts to write a coherent and well-substantiated life of Jesus and the rise of Form-criticism, which has left virtually every statement in the Gospels open to question, this problem has become one of desperate urgency for the church. It, more than anything else, has been the cause of those modern attenuations of the Gospel[1] which drastically reduce the area of belief in order to provide a more defensible perimeter. Among all but a very sophisticated minority, this is a form of apologetic which has produced more bewilderment than conviction.

Pannenberg reverses this trend in two respects. Firstly, he makes an ally instead of an enemy out of critical history. Secondly, he restores the area of belief to something like its original

---

[1] Cf. H. D. Lewis, *Philosophy of Religion* (English Universities Press, 1965), 113 ff.

proportions. This is good apologetic. Christianity will never come to terms with the modern world until it can defend its historical components on historical grounds (rather than distilling them into existential or other non-historical doctrines). It will not be credible as Christianity unless it retains the traditional substance of the faith.

But can Pannenberg perform this *tour de force*? Can the subjective certainty of faith be made compatible with the objective probabilities of history? Pannenberg answers this question in two moves, one logical, the other psychological. The first is that the concept of certainty needs to be used carefully and critically. 'Certainty' is always relative to the realm of discourse in which it is applied. For example, a mathematical statement has a different kind of certainty from a statement of empirical science. There is no such thing as absolute certainty this side of omniscience. Even in formal logic one can be mistaken.

Historical statements have their own kind of certainty to which they may in varying degrees approximate. Pannenberg accepts Otto Kirn's statement of this,

> 'A historical conclusion can be regarded as certain when . . . despite the fact that it is not removed from all possible attack, it is nevertheless in agreement with all the known facts.' [2]

But many of the most important historical statements in the New Testament do not attain to even this kind of certainty. Statements, for instance, about what Jesus thought and said, are, in the present light of source criticism, at best probable. Pannenberg accepts source-critical methods and frequently acknowledges that assertions about the original teaching of Jesus are only probable. Yet there are points at which his theology has to depend heavily on establishing the authenticity of certain of the sayings of Jesus.

His solution is, firstly, to distinguish faith very sharply from the knowledge on which it is based. Secondly, he distinguishes

[2] Pannenberg, *Basic Questions*, Vol. I, p. 54.

sharply between the logical and the psychological relations of faith and knowledge. Merely probable knowledge is psychologically compatible with the trustful certainty of faith. A man may take a balanced, critical view of the arguments for and against the resurrection of Jesus as an historical event. He may, at the same time believe trustfully and wholeheartedly that this ultimate demonstration of God's trustworthiness did occur.

There is nothing illogical or unreasonable in the combination of such trust with merely probable knowledge. The analogy of marriage is over-worked in the sphere of religion. But it is useful again in this case. A man, after reading the Kinsey report, may be objectively aware that there is a statistical probability that his wife is being unfaithful to him. This knowledge is both psychologically and logically compatible with a trusting belief that she is in fact faithful.

This does not make faith independent of knowledge. Trust where there were no rational grounds for belief would be sheer irresponsibility. But faith is compatible with the degree of uncertainty inherent not only in historical knowledge, but in all finite, human knowledge. Pannenberg thus steers a middle course between the attempt, on the one hand, to make faith secure by divorcing it from factual knowledge altogether and, on the other hand, to make it rest upon 'infallible' truths.[3]

DIRECT AND INDIRECT SELF-DISCLOSURE

To sustain this account of the relation between history and faith, the distinction between direct and indirect disclosure must be strictly maintained. Stories about theophanies or 'personal appearances' of God or the gods are not uncommon in religions

---

[3] In its broad outlines this solution seems so obvious that one wonders why it has not been more seriously considered during the past two hundred years. Pannenberg claims no novelty for it. He suggests that this relation between historical knowledge and faith is precisely that intended by the Reformers in their distinction between *notitia* and *assensus* on the one hand and *fiducia* on the other. (See *Basic Questions*, Vol. II, pp. 30 ff.)

This solution fits well with his account of the relation of faith and reason, for which he also claims the support of Luther. (See *Basic Questions*, Vol. I, pp. 61 ff.)

generally. These would count as direct self-disclosures. What appears in such disclosures is identical with the essence of the God. The appearance need not be visual to be direct. It may be an auditory self-disclosure—a divine oracle. Such direct disclosures are a common feature of pagan religions.

In contrast with this, the notion of a God who discloses himself in events which are part of the day to day course of history, because these events are thought of as the outcome of his actions, involves indirect self-disclosure. God is not identified with or necessarily present in the medium of disclosure.

This distinction is quite fundamental to Pannenberg's doctrine of revelation as history. He illustrates it by reference to the difference between direct and indirect *communication*. Of this he says:

'Direct communication has in an immediate way just that content that it intends to communicate, whereas indirect communication initially has some other content than that which is actually to be communicated.' [4]

This is helpful so far as it goes; but there are many different kinds of indirect communication. It would have been helpful if Pannenberg had given us a fuller analysis. For example, a broad hint would fit the above description as an instance of indirect communication. If, in the weeks prior to his birthday, a man were to talk frequently to his family of his admiration for a particular type of fishing rod, that would be a form of indirect communication. But I do not find in that any analogy which helps me to understand the nature of the divine self-disclosure in the biblical tradition. Such deliberately veiled hinting is clearly not what is intended.

On the other hand there are some relationships in which indirect communication seems to play an integral and indispensable role. This is particularly so where trust and personal relation is involved. For example, friendship is not usually expressed by

---

[4] Pannenberg, *Revelation as History*, p. 14.

saying 'I am your friend' (except by the confidence trickster). It is usually expressed indirectly. It comes to expression in the relationship itself as it is lived and experienced.

If Pannenberg had given a closer analysis of the exact sense in which indirect communication is involved in the biblical tradition and why such a form of communication is peculiarly appropriate to the self-disclosure of the God of Israel, his position would have been more readily understandable. He would also have saved himself from what seem to me to be mistaken judgements which he passed upon some of the theologies of personal encounter (based on Ferdinand Ebner and Martin Buber and others). He condemns these as 'gnostic' theologies based on direct communication. Both Buber and Ebner are, I should have thought, fully aware of the essentially indirect character of the I–Thou relation.

As Pannenberg freely acknowledges, the Old Testament does recognize appearances of the God of Israel which reflect the tradition of direct theophanies in the religion of the ancient Near East. But he is fully justified in asserting (with the support of Rolf Rendtorff) [5] that in the form in which we have received the tradition, these have sunk into relative unimportance and are to be interpreted in the light of a dominant belief in the indirect self-manifestation of God through history.

Attempts have been made to give the notion of a direct self-communication of God in revelation a more prominent place in the Old Testament. It has been alleged that such direct self-disclosure of God is to be found in the communication of the divine name to Moses on Mt Sinai, or in the communication of the law, or in the notion of the Word of God revealed to and through the prophets. But this Pannenberg rejects as a misinterpretation of the Israelite tradition. To interpret the disclosure of the divine name as a direct self-disclosure of Jahweh is to import into the story pagan conceptions (that the essential being of God is contained in his name) which are foreign to it. To interpret the giving of the law as a direct disclosure of the will of God would

[5] *Ibid.*, p. 23 ff.

involve identifying the covenant law with the will of God. This would mean that it could never be changed to meet changing circumstance.

But what is wrong with a direct disclosure of God's person in revelation apart from the fact that it is characteristically pagan and gnostic? Perhaps the pagans and gnostics were right.

The main objections to the notion of revelation as the direct self-disclosure of God are: Firstly, it posits a simple identity of the divine with the object or event in which the disclosure takes place. It is thus an idolatrous concept. Secondly, in its direct character it makes the divinity of God wholly plain to those who are 'in the know'—the initiates. This is its gnostic character. Thirdly, since in its direct character it involves a total disclosure of the divine either in the past or the present, it leaves no room for real openness and anticipated novelty in the future. It leaves history with no further meaning. This is where both paganism and gnosticism are at fault in comparison with the central biblical tradition.

FAITH AND KNOWLEDGE

For modern man the most attractive feature of the notion of *indirect* self-disclosure of God in history is that it offers relief from the sort of supernaturalism which, ever since the Enlightenment, we have nearly all felt to be somewhat offensive. There is no oracle of God announcing secret truths. There are no supernatural events which are isolated from the rest of history as unambiguous appearances or acts of the deity. God's self-disclosure takes place within the continuity of the world's ordinary happenings. It can be approached in the same spirit of rationality as we employ in any other branch of knowledge.

It is this continuity with the rest of the world's happening and its openness to rational enquiry from every quarter that distinguishes the indirect self-disclosure of God in history from all other senses of revelation. It does not require faith as a means of access to knowledge but requires knowledge and sound judgement as a basis for faith. The truth of the revelation is open to all. This, ultimately, is what distinguishes it absolutely from 'gnosticism'.

Even when Jahweh was still thought of only as the God of Israel, he was believed to be demonstrating his deity *to all peoples*. Pannenberg quotes an anti-gnostic passage from 2 Cor. 4:2 in support of his position: 'By the *open* statement of the truth [Τῃ φανερώσει της ἀληθείας] we would commend ourselves to every man's conscience in the sight of God'.[6] There is no secret knowledge here which is not open to rational inspection.

It has often been suggested that the inspiration of the Holy Spirit is encessary as a pre-condition for insight into the meaning of the revealing events. This is usually based on such texts as 'No man can say that Jesus is Lord, but by the Holy Ghost' (1 Cor. 12:3). This suggestion is also rejected by Pannenberg[7] in his insistence on the openness of historic revelation to normal, critical investigation. With the support of Bultmann he insists that Paul never describes faith as a gift of the Spirit, but rather that the Spirit is the gift received in and with faith. In any case, faith as *fiducia* is the commitment to what rational insight perceives in the events. It is not itself an organ of perception. 'A revelation', Pannenberg says, 'that requires supplementation to be manifest is not yet a true revelation.'[8]

But to say that knowledge of revelation is not supernatural does not mean that man is only confirming what he already knows. A real disclosure takes place. God has shown who he is in what Pannenberg calls 'the language of facts'. The events of the history of Israel, culminating in the death and resurrection of Jesus, are very special events in this respect. But their special character lies in the events themselves, not in the attitude or inspiration with which one confronts them.

What role does faith play then? 'Faith is not a state of blissful gullibility.'[9] Faith is a way of facing life—particularly of facing life's future—on the basis of the lessons learned from the revealing

[6] Cf. *Ibid.*, p. 136.
[8] *Ibid.*, p. 19.
[7] *Ibid.*, pp, 19, 136 f., 195 f.
[9] *Ibid.*, p. 138.

events of history. It is trust in the promises of God discerned in that history and a hopefully expectant attitude to the future on the basis of these promises. It is not the knowledge of revelation itself, but the consequent faith in God that secures salvation.

But while the logical relation between faith and knowledge is such that faith is always consequent upon knowledge, this is not true of their psychological relation. A man may be blinded to the true meaning of events by prejudice and preconception. He may hold these prejudices and preconceptions in the name of rationality. They may, in fact, be a distortion of rational open-mindedness. A good deal of modern positivism has this character. Even the most rudimentary elements of faith can break through the prison of such prejudice and preconception. In this respect faith can become an aid to rationality and not merely a consequence of it.

THE HISTORY OF ISRAEL AS THE SELF-DISCLOSURE OF GOD

Since God is the creator of all, then every aspect of creation and every event of history is a disclosure of his being. But in the tradition of all peoples certain events emerge as key events for the interpretation of the rest. This was so within the tradition of Israel. In the outworking of the history of that tradition it has become the key for interpreting much that lies outside it.

Granted that events may have meaning, how does such meaning come to be interpreted as the self-revelation of God?

Pannenberg acknowledges two main grounds for this in the tradition of the Old Testament. An event may qualify for recognition as an act of God—and therefore as an indirect self-disclosure—(1) because of its unpredictable, radical novelty,[10] (2) because it fulfills an expectation aroused by previous history (a promise of God).[11]

[10] *Basic Questions*, Vol. I, pp. 48, 76; *Ibid.*, Vol. II, pp. 113 ff.
[11] *Revelation as History*, pp. 128 ff.

On the face of it these two grounds seem to contradict one another. The one rests on unpredictability, the other on prediction. But the relation between them is much more complex than that of simple contradiction.

In terms of the first of the above principles, God is thought of as the source of radical novelty in history. It is the novel, the contingent, the unforeseeable which distinguishes history from nature. This novelty raises the question of the creative source of the 'new thing' that has come to pass. When again and again the people of Israel found themselves led into new and unforeseeable circumstances, again and again unpredictably delivered from their enemies or the improbable victors in a struggle, they felt impelled to say, 'This is the Lord's doing and it is marvellous in our eyes.' (Psalms 118: 23.) This way of seeing the novel and contingent in history is directly related to a distinctively Israelite way of conceiving of the creativity, freedom and transcendence of God.

In this connection the distinction between direct and indirect revelation is important. In early Canaanite religion and in the ancient Near East generally, the transcendence of the gods was thought of as exalted isolation from human affairs. Their permanent association with the earth was not through history. (The very concept of history as we know it had scarcely come into being.) It was through the natural processes with which they were associated—the heavenly bodies, the vegetation cycle, and so on —that they were known. The essence of such associations lies in the regularity of the cycle, the absence of novelty. When such gods disclose themselves it is in an isolated manifestation of their 'glory'—an event unrelated to what has gone before and what is coming after. It is an incursion into human affairs, independent of and unrelated to the course of history. In these circumstances no conception of history as independent of nature and in itself significant for the gods could arise.

It has already been acknowledged that in the earliest strata of the tradition of Israel we find traces of the same conception of a God who discloses himself in direct epiphanies. But this was, at

a very early stage, overlaid by the conception that God is indirectly revealed in the course of human affairs.

With this a new conception of *significant* history arose. It was
the direct correlate of a new conception of God as independent
of natural process. God became transcendent in a new sense. His
transcendence does not consist in his exalted status in the glory
of the divine realm (though the old symbolism continues in the
new context). It consists in his power to bring forth what is new
and marvellous in the course of human affairs.

Of course, what is referred to here is not mere novelty. It is
not sheer contingency. That in itself would be no different in its
significance from the isolated epiphanies of direct revelation.
Significant novelty is not a mere bolt from the blue but something
positively related to what has gone before and what comes after.
It shows the past in a new light and opens new questions for the
future.

Thus, when the people of Israel made their escape from Egypt
across the Red Sea, an undreamed-of possibility was realized
and an unimaginable new future opened up before them. Something absolutely new which was not a simple development of its
historical antecedents had taken place. Yet it was something
which could be related to their traditional past. This marvellous
thing that had happened was ascribed to a God who transcended
all the powers inherent in the present and the past (and thus
transcended all known conceptions of the divine).

This God was at the same time identified with the God of
Abraham, of Isaac and of Jacob. But this was not a simple identification; for the God of the patriarchs was now seen in an entirely
new light. The ancient promises, recorded in the tradition of
Israel, had been fulfilled in a way which would certainly have
surprised the patriarchs. Yet this had come to pass in a way
which, after the event, was recognizably a fulfilment of the
promises.

This gives a clue to the relation between the two apparently contradictory criteria for the recognition of an event as a
revelatory act of God. The first criterion is the radical novelty

of the event—its unforeseeable character. The second is its recognition as fulfilling the expectations raised by previous events—expectations which were interpreted as the promises of God in previous self-disclosures. The two criteria are not incompatible, as might at first appear.

Novelty which was mere novelty and contingency which was mere contingency could only have revealed a god of sheer whim and caprice. A history which was mere unambiguous fulfilment of expectations arising out of the past could disclose only a god bound to nature like the *baalim* of ancient Canaan. In neither case could the god so disclosed give rise to the concept of history as it arose out of Israel's experience. Only if novelty and contingency are significantly and positively related to predictability and expectation can the idea of history as we know it arise.

The dialectic of the two criteria by which the history of Israel is recognized as the self-disclosure of Jahweh—surprise on the one hand and fulfilment of expectation on the other—corresponds to the deepest problem of modern historiography. This is the problem of how to combine recognition of the continuity and unity of history with an equal recognition of the elements of contingency, novelty and openness of the future, without which history would not be history. In order to be fit subjects for rational investigation historical events must be explicable or understandable in terms of their relation to the total complex of which they form a part. Otherwise no understanding of the past or rational expectation for the future would be possible. That is to say, history is conceived as a complex within which events are explicable in terms of their antecedents and the future can be anticipated by reference to the past. (This corresponds to the element of expectation and fulfilment in the Israelite understanding of their own history.) On the other hand, to be distinguishable from nature, history must contain an element of novelty, surprise, contingency and creativity. (This corresponds to the Israelite belief in the free, creative and transcendent activity of Jahweh in their history.)

In a difficult and sometimes obscure section of his essay on

'Redemptive Event and History' [12] Pannenberg argues that the dilemma of modern secular historiography is that it cannot accommodate those two elements. Only the distinctive traditio-historical dialectic which develops in Israel from the recognition of history as the self-disclosure of Jahweh has been able to do so. In a bold new apologetic, Pannenberg therefore argues that:

> 'Since only the concept of God makes it possible to conceive the unity of history in a way that maintains the peculiar characteristics of the historical, it should really be indispensable for the historian.' [13]

Alone among the nations Israel was enabled to see history neither as sheer caprice of the gods nor as part of nature. Its end is not deducible from its beginning. It is open towards the future in a way which corresponds to man's openness beyond his world. Its sense rests upon the constancy of God.

Thus the significance of the past or present is never exhaustively disclosed in its occurrence. Future events may disclose its deeper meaning. History itself thus forms the tradition which supplies the context in which each new event is experienced. The significance of each new event reflects in turn upon the tradition. Each new marvel requires a 'new song'; but the new song celebrates a deeper level at which the old tradition is understood in the light of the new event.

> 'O sing to the Lord a new song; for he has done marvellous things: his right hand and his holy arm, have gotten him the victory.
> The Lord has made known his victory, He has revealed his vindication in the sight of the nations.
> He has remembered his steadfast love and his faithfulness to the house of Israel.' (Psalms 98:1–3.)

The concept of the *universal* sovereignty of God emerged only gradually in Israel. With it there arose the concept of universal

---

[12] *Basic Questions*, Vol. I, pp. 15–80. See especially pp. 66 ff.
[13] *Ibid.*, p. 76.

history. At first Canaan was the world of Israel. It was enough that God ruled there. The sovereignty of God was sufficiently demonstrated in the meaning they found in their local history. Their struggles with the Canaanite tribes and with the Philistines were interpreted in terms of their traditions about Jahweh. But equally, these events illuminated and transformed their traditions about Jahweh.

When Israel became a contender for control of the international caravan routes under David, and a contender in international trade under Solomon, a new understanding of God emerged in and with a new and wider understanding of their history.

It was under the succession of 'world' empires from the period of the Exile onwards that the idea of the universal sovereignty of God became explicit. It arose *pari passu* with the idea of universal history. The final expression of this was in the apocalyptic tradition. Pannenberg finds an underlying unity in all the varied strands of apocalyptic writing. It is the theme that the meaning of history will be fully known only when the end of history has come and all is disclosed. Then both the justice and the glory of God will be disclosed and his divinity and universal sovereignty vindicated. In the meantime the events of history are the self-disclosure of God only indirectly and in anticipation of the end.

This emphasis on universal history does not eliminate the particularity of the revelation of God as it occurred specifically in the history of Israel. It is only in the context of the *expectation* (arising from tradition) of God's future action in history that events have the character of divine self-disclosure. It was in Israel that this happened. But it happened in a way which refers to the whole of history. It is from the perspective of the tradition and history of Israel that this distinctive concept of universal history arose.

Pannenberg would, of course, concede that other conceptions of universal 'history' did arise from sources independent of Israel. There was, for instance, the view prevalent in classical culture, of history as a cyclical process involving recession from an original golden age and an eventual return. But Pannenberg would want to put inverted commas round the word 'history' as used here. It does not have the distinctive sense of history that has come down to us through the Judaeo-Christian tradition and which has become a permanent element in our culture. This conception of history, he would claim, is uniquely Jewish and Christian in its origins. It has a pre-eminent validity; for it alone can accommodate the openness, the radical novelty and the contingency of our future along with the concept of universal meaning of history and the fulfilment of destiny. This corresponds with man's openness in hope beyond the world and so can answer the question of God that arises out of our historical existence.

It was the apocalyptic tradition which provided the context for Jesus and his message.

Chapter 4

THE APOCALYPTIC CONTEXT
OF JESUS AND HIS MESSAGE

Christology, as Pannenberg sees it, is not about some celestial transaction but is the interpretation of an historical event. It should not be approached with the presupposition that God became incarnate in Jesus Christ. That is something which should be allowed to emerge from the meaning of the event itself. The doctrine should be understood in a sense determined by the event itself. In this sense christology must always be approached from 'below'.

Such an historical approach can yield doctrinal conclusions because the meaning of the event is inherent within it and open to historical reason. It is not a secret 'inner' meaning open only to the initiate. All one needs to approach it is an honest mind free from prejudice. The godhead is not veiled or hidden in the historic flesh of Jesus, but is made manifest in it. It is the climactic and absolute point in the self-disclosure of God within history. But even in this case the mode of disclosure is indirect. This indirectness is the only element of truth reflected in the doctrine that the flesh (the historic existence) of the Christ is also a veiling of his godhead.

Any event in history has meaning only in relation to the traditio-historical context within which it takes place. Its relation to its own context belongs inherently to it. The context of the action and destiny of Jesus is one of apocalyptic expectation. This fact has emerged with more clarity and certainty than any other in the course of modern New Testament studies.

The Apocalyptic Context of Jesus and His Message

It is a fact which has occasioned a good deal of embarrassment. The early nineteenth-century lives of Jesus endeavoured to present him in terms which modern Europe could understand. His person was interpreted in terms of his moral character and the kingdom he proclaimed in terms of progressive moral education. The re-discovery of the apocalyptic setting of the life and teaching of Jesus—especially through the work of Johannes Weiss and Albert Schweitzer—changed all that. It brought home how foreign Jesus, his manner of thought and his times are to us.[1]

However mixed its origins, the apocalyptic tradition, by the time of Jesus had become something distinctively Jewish. It belonged mainly to the relatively brief inter-Testamental period. From the very start it proved an embarrassment to the church. The rest of the world did not know what to make of it. To the Greeks it was a laughing stock (though many of the Greek-speaking Fathers—especially Origen—were to display marvellous ingenuity in translating it into terms of Middle Platonism and late Stoic philosophy). The Gnostics spiritualized it in a symbolic interpretation. The West, under the influence of St Augustine, finally placed a largely ecclesiological interpretation upon it in terms of the relation between the heavenly and the earthly city.

It became clear in the historical studies of the nineteenth century that none of these interpretations, ingenious though they were, really measured up to the original meaning and intention of Jewish apocalyptic. But the apocalyptic vision of the end of the world, final judgement, general resurrection of the dead in the body, and the establishment of a new heaven and a new earth is so foreign to our whole way of thinking that we can scarcely participate sympathetically in it even in the wildest flights of our imagination. As a result, most of the very considerable ingenuity of New Testament scholarship for over a century has been devoted to attempts to divorce the meaning of Jesus and his

[1] Pannenberg, *Theology and the Kingdom of God*, pp. 52 ff.

message from its strange apocalyptic setting. The climax of this movement was reached in Bultmann's de-mythologizing programme and his existentialist interpretation of the Gospel.

Pannenberg reverses this trend completely. Again and again one finds this—that it is as a reverser of trends that he stands in such a strategically significant position in modern theology. We have already seen how the apparently damaging effects of modern critical history on the Gospel led to a flight from history into the theology of faith in response to the divinely authoritative Word. Pannenberg made an ally rather than an enemy out of critical history. Similarly, instead of treating the apocalyptic context of the life and teaching of Jesus as an embarrassment from which the essential message and meaning must be detached, he welcomes it positively into his thought as the very heart and essence of the message.

The apocalyptic literature of the inter-Testamental period is far from uniform. It represents quite a wide spectrum of theological opinion about the final advent of the kingdom of God. However, certain broad features are pervasive. It is with these rather than the variegated detail that Pannenberg concerns himself. He abstracts three ideas as of primary significance.

1. Although God discloses himself in the history of Israel, it is only at the end of history that the disclosure is complete and the divinity, justice and constancy of God are fully revealed.

2. This end of history is significant not only for the Jewish people (though they play a special role in relation to that consummation). It is the final event in which God is vindicated as the God of all peoples and of all creation. It is of universal significance. Therefore it is not so foreign and incomprehensible to people of other times and cultures as might first appear.

3. The concept of the end of history, in order that all history may be summed up in it, involves a general resurrection of the dead.

Pannenberg is justified in singling out these ideas as of primary importance within the apocalyptic tradition. But it should be realized that this is an emphasis arising largely from a Christian perspective on apocalyptic. It could not be accepted as an historical account of what appeared to the people of Jesus own day as the most important or the defining characteristics of apocalyptic generally. Indeed the whole question of the nature and extent of the role played by apocalyptic thought in the Judaism of Jesus' day is still one of the most vexing problems in the history of religions. Pannenberg looks at apocalyptic not only through a Christian window, but a window that has been double-glazed with materials drawn from Greek philosophy and German Idealism.

On this score one might criticize him for neglect of the purely historical method which he is otherwise so anxious to advocate. However, such criticism would be at least partly based on a misunderstanding of what he means by historical method. He does not propose to abandon theology to the mercies of the positivist historian as he is currently known. The typical historian of religion is content to show, so far as he can, what apocalyptic contained and how it was understood within inter-Testamental Judaism. In Pannenberg's view this is a wrong approach to history. It is not enough to know what apocalyptic writings meant for people 'then'. To understand any historical phenomenon properly you also need to know what it became in its later out-working. (That is one of the lessons that apocalyptic has to teach the historian.) Therefore Pannenberg is prepared to look at apocalyptic not in a merely antiquarian way but from his own perspective as a man who knows what it became, *through the action and fate of Jesus,* in the hands of the Greek Fathers, of Augustine, of Joachim of Floris, of the Reformers, of Hegel, Marx and nineteenth-century historiographers. This, in his view, is what a historical understanding of a phenomenon really involves.[2]

On these grounds he is justified in taking up the notion of the

[2] This is something that has to be kept in mind when Pannenberg is criticized for trying to make history do too much for theology (e.g. G. O'Collins, in *Foundations of Theology* (Gill and Macmillan, 1971), pp. 115 ff.). He is proposing an approach to history altogether different from that of current historical method.

end of the 'age' in apocalyptic as that of the *completion* of history. He is correct in interpreting the cosmic scope of apocalyptic imagery as representing the unity of universal history under God. These are post-Hegelian concepts. But they arise directly from the out-working of the apocalyptic context of the life and action of Jesus—even though it may be seriously doubted whether they were the first thoughts in the mind of a first-century Jew in that connection.

JESUS' RELATION TO THE APOCALYPTIC TRADITION

This is another of the very difficult problems of New Testament history which Pannenberg handles with remarkably cavalier confidence. But he is almost, if not wholly, successful in justifying this confidence. In the past, when attempts have been made to settle the christological question on the basis of historical research the issues have usually turned on questions about the self-consciousness of Jesus or whether christological titles such as Son of Man, Son of God, Messiah and so on were applied to him before or after his death, and whether he accepted or acknowledged such titles and if so, in what sense. Historical christology has been in a state of crisis for over a hundred years because, even with the best of modern critical methods, it has proved impossible to answer these questions with any confidence. Or rather, for every confident affirmation there has been an equally confident counter-affirmation.

Pannenberg fully supports the application of modern critical methods to Scripture. Where the results are uncertain he does not over-play his hand. He has views on the difficult issues mentioned above which he states with appropriate caution and with reference to the differences of opinion among the best of modern scholars.

However, on the basis of his 'streamlining' of what he takes to be the primary characteristics of apocalyptic, he is able to narrow down the area of historical decision which is crucial for christology to far more manageable limits. For him the vital historical affirmations about Jesus which are essential for christological doctrine are:

1. Jesus came proclaiming the imminence of the Kingdom of God in a context of apocalyptic expectation.

2. He taught that the fate of individuals in the final judgement would be determined by their relation to him and his message. (In this he departed from the common apocalyptic tradition that the fate of each individual in the last judgement would depend on whether he had kept the law.)

3. Jesus rose from the dead. This was an objective event openly witnessed by all who had access to the evidence (the resurrection appearances and the empty tomb).

These three assertions are central to Pannenberg's theology. He is prepared to defend each of them on grounds wholly drawn from historical argument.

The first is hardly in dispute. I think it will be generally agreed that only a very perverse and ideologically motivated scepticism would deny that the Jesus of the scriptural tradition did have a historical prototype and that he proclaimed the coming of God's Kingdom in a context of apocalyptic expectation.

The second is a very much more tricky historical question. It raises the question of the claims of Jesus. This is one which more than a hundred years of intensive historical research and literary criticism of the documents has been unable to settle. However, Pannenberg does ease the situation by minimizing the amount of historical information necessary to sustain his argument. He does not require any precise information about the nature of Jesus' claim to authority. He does not need to know whether he claimed to be Messiah or Son of God or Son of Man. It is enough for Pannenberg to establish that he did make a claim to authority and a demand for decision in relation to his person and message within a context of apocalyptic expectation. The true nature of Jesus' claim to authority and call to decision did not and could not become clear until the resurrection. There is therefore no attempt to establish the divinity of Jesus on the basis of his pre-Easter history. (This was the weakness of former attempts to found christology on history.) All that the pre-Easter history need contain is some claim which, no matter how deeply implicit, is made explicit, interpreted and confirmed in the resurrection.

By what is more than a happy coincidence this is as much as the most critical modern New Testament scholars are willing to concede. Even Bultmann, who goes further than most in treating every christological claim on the lips of Jesus as a theological invention of the early church, is willing to concede that 'in his lifetime he had demanded decision for his person as the bearer of the Word . . . Jesus' call to decision implies a christology'. [3] This has been taken up even more strongly by the post-Bultmann school. Thus Pannenberg can quote E. Käsemann saying, 'Only if Jesus' proclamation decisively coincides with the proclamation about Jesus is it understandable, reasonable and necessary that the Christian kerygma in the New Testament conceals the message of Jesus; only then is the resurrected Jesus the historical Jesus.' [4] He receives further support for the view that Jesus' words and conduct implied some claim to be the one who ushers in the apocalyptic 'end-time' from Ernst Fuchs, Günther Bornkamm and Hans Conzelmann (though they would not all support his interpretation in detail). He may reasonably claim the support of the general trend in New Testament scholarship. In the new quest for the historical Jesus which has arisen since Bultmann stress is laid not so much on the difference between Jesus and the apostolic preaching—as was the case in the liberal quest for the historical Jesus—but rather on the continuity between the apostolic message and Jesus himself.

Contemporary New Testament scholars (especially those of the Bultmann school) are in varying degrees inclined to differ from Pannenberg's emphasis on the futurity of the kingdom of God. This is an old problem. There are two strands in the teaching of Jesus. One suggests that the Kingdom of God is already present. The

[3] R. Bultmann, *Theology of the New Testament* (S.C.M.P., 1971), Vol. I, p. 43.
[4] E. Käsemann, 'Probleme neutestamentlicher Arbeit in Deutschland', in *Die Freiheit des Evangeliums und die Ordnung der Gesellschaft*, p. 151, cf. Pannenberg, *Jesus—God and Man*, p. 56.

other points to its coming in a future cataclysmic event. No systematic interpretation of the Gospels has ever succeeded entirely in eliminating this tension. Pannenberg places Jesus' teaching firmly within the traditional apocalyptic context in this respect. In his view Jesus confidently expected the imminent coming of the Kingdom as a future event. Many New Testament scholars resist this conclusion. But their reasons for doing so are often more theological than historical. Historically there are strong grounds for thinking that Jesus thought in those terms. But so long as one thinks that the apocalyptic tradition is unintelligible to all but first-century Jews, there is a strong theological motive for resisting this conclusion. It would mean that the central message of Jesus must remain for ever foreign to us. But Pannenberg is firmly of the opinion that modern man may still picture his world and its destiny within an apocalyptic framework without any anachronism. Once this difficulty is overcome the case for a thoroughly apocalyptic interpretation of the self-understanding and expectation of Jesus is greatly strengthened.

The initial likelihood is that Jesus would share the traditions and thought-forms of his own time.

An emphasis on the futurity of the Kingdom of God has the systematic advantage that it establishes definite truth-conditions for the claims of Jesus. If the apocalyptic expectations are in one way or another fulfilled, then the claims are to that extent vindicated. If they are not fulfilled, then the claims are false. On the other hand, if one places all the emphasis on Jesus' claim that the Kingdom is already present in him then in the last resort his claim has to be self-authenticating.

In this connection Pannenberg lays special stress on the saying from the 'Q' source in the form recorded in Luke 12:8 (cf. Matthew 10:32 f.): 'And I tell you, everyone who acknowledges me before men, the Son of Man shall also acknowledge before the angels of God.' The case for the authenticity of this saying is very strong. The fact that Jesus does not identify himself with the divine Son of Man, who is still to come, strongly counters the suggestion that this saying is the result of theological elaboration in the early church. (That influence is typically at work in the Matthean version, where 'Son of Man' is replaced by 'I'.)

Pannenberg succeeds in combining the claim to ultimate, divine significance with a credible and moving humanity in Jesus. He agrees with Schweitzer to the extent that he acknowledges the thoroughly apocalyptic form of the self-understanding and the message of Jesus. But he differs radically from Schweitzer in that he does not treat this apocalyptic message as something totally foreign to our way of thinking and doomed to final disillusionment even in Jesus himself. The claim of Jesus to apocalyptic significance is vindicated in the resurrection in a way which gives it meaning and validity within all cultures.

I find his account of Jesus' progress towards his fate both humanly credible and deeply moving (more so than Schweitzer's somewhat hysterical account of the same events).

'Only when one sees that the question of the ultimate confirmation of Jesus' claim to authority stands over his entire path does one understand the point of the journey to Jerusalem. Jesus apparently was determined to bring about a decision. That he virtually forced a decision seems to be suggested by the narrative of the cleansing of the temple [Mark 11:15–19 and parallels], at least the kernel of which may be historical.

From this point of view it would be very peculiar if Jesus had not reckoned at least with the possibility of his death in Jerusalem, though not in the sense of the predictions of the passion in the Gospels, which are certainly *vaticinia ex eventu*, as has been generally accepted since Wrede. Nevertheless, his journey to Jerusalem was certainly no deed of despair. Jesus probably expected that God would, in one way or another, acknowledge him, even in the case of his own failure. This assumption is all the less to be rejected, since Jesus in any case reckoned with the imminent end of the world and the resurrection of the dead and judgment of the Son of Man which were associated with that. Measured by the imminent nearness of these events of the end, it must have been of secondary significance for Jesus whether he himself would have to endure death before the end came. The truth of his proclamation did not need to depend on this. One way or the other the ultimate confirmation of his message through the imminent fulfilment of all history with the appearance of the Son of Man on the clouds of heaven was immediately at hand. This occurrence of the end, however, must bring the verification of his authority.'

He goes on to summarize his position as follows:

'There is no reason for the assumption that Jesus' claim to authority taken by itself justified faith in him. On the contrary, the pre-Easter Jesus' claim to authority stands from the beginning in relationship to the question of the future verification of his message through the occurrence of the future judgment of the Son of Man according to the attitude taken by men toward Jesus. Thus has been shown the proleptic structure of Jesus' claim to authority, which is analogous to that of the Old Testament prophetic sayings. This means, however, that Jesus' claim to authority by itself cannot be made the basis of a Christology, as though this only involved the 'decision' in relation to him. Such Christology—and the preaching based upon it—would remain an empty assertion. Rather, everything depends upon the connection between Jesus' claim and its confirmation by God.'[5]

[5] *Jesus—God and Man*, pp. 65–6.

Chapter 5

RESURRECTION—THE FACT AND ITS MEANING

In placing the emphasis he does on the future vindication of the claims of Jesus, Pannenberg stakes everything on the resurrection. As an historical question this is the trickiest of all. But before we tackle the historical question as such certain preparatory remarks need to be made.

Firstly, Pannenberg's position, vulnerable though it is to both historical and philosophical criticism, is in agreement with the earliest strata of the Christian tradition in placing such an emphasis on the resurrection. 'If Christ be not raised your faith is vain and ye are still in your sins.' (1 Cor. 15 : 17.)

Secondly, the meaning of the resurrection events within the context of apocalyptic expectation must be made clear. That meaning is quite definite. If Jesus was raised from the dead, then the end of the world has begun. For Jesus' Jewish contemporaries, in so far as they shared the apocalyptic expectation, the resurrection of Jesus did not need to be interpreted. If such a thing had happened, then it spoke for itself.

Admittedly the apocalyptic tradition spoke of a general resurrection. It did not predict any foretaste of this. But if the event happened then it could be interpreted only as such a foretaste.

Thus interpreted it wholly vindicated the claims of Jesus. This in turn could only mean that the final disclosure of the glory, the justice and the constancy of God, destined to occur at the end of the world, is already anticipated in Jesus Christ. Translated into Greek concepts this means that Jesus is identical with the divine

70

logos. This is the route by which christology as the doctrine of the divinity of Christ arises out of the resurrection understood in relation to its apocalyptic context.

Thirdly, we need to get the concept of the resurrection of the dead into correct perspective before we can tackle the historical problem openly and objectively. If one approaches the historical question about the resurrection of Jesus with a wrong conception of what it means or on the basis of the assumption that the dead do not rise, then the enquiry is prejudiced from the outset.

Resurrection, in the context of Jewish apocalyptic, should be clearly distinguished from the concept of immortality of the soul. Unfortunately, in forming its ideas about what lies beyond death the whole of Christendom has been deeply influenced by the Greek concept of immortality of the soul. This concept has been entertained mainly in the form given it by Plato. The soul is thought to be immortal because, being intellectual in character, it has affinity with eternal ideas and is therefore not subject to change. The strong influence of this concept has impeded proper understanding and appreciation of the biblical concept of resurrection. The Greek concept of immortality has become incredible to modern man, Pannenberg thinks. As a result the biblical concept of resurrection has also become incredible without being properly understood or given a proper hearing. The Greek concept has become incredible firstly because we now understand our world in terms of the processes going on in it rather than a changeless substratum; and secondly because physiology and allied sciences have made the idea of a life-soul existing apart from the body virtually inconceivable.[1]

Once the Jewish concept of resurrection is clearly differentiated

[1] If Pannenberg is here merely describing a *de facto* sociological and cultural situation, then what he says is beyond dispute. But if he is suggesting, as he seems to be, that modern man is correct in rejecting the notion of immortality of the soul for these reasons, then he is relying on a singularly weak argument. The ground for rejecting the Greek concept must ultimately be neither sociological nor scientific but philosophical. Any considered rejection of the concept of immortality of the soul in the modern world would have to take as much account of Descartes as of Plato. I cannot avoid the opinion that Pannenberg suffers here, as in many other places from his reluctance to leave the historical–critical level and become fully engaged in metaphysics.

from the Greek concept of immortality, Pannenberg argues, it can be seen to be both credible and relevant to contemporary thought. In the first place, it does not separate soul and body but speaks of resurrection of the body. This would not in itself be any more credible to modern man until one realizes that, secondly: this does not refer in a literal and grossly mythological way to the resuscitation and revivification of mouldering corpses.[2] It is a symbolic conception. The basic metaphor is that of rising up from sleep, of awakening. But of what is it symbolic? We know only the metaphor. The reality is unknown.

> 'The familiar experience of being awakened and rising from sleep serves as a parable for the *completely unknown* destiny expected for the dead.'[3]

I have drawn special attention to the words 'completely unknown' here for two reasons. Firstly, it is important that the sense in which the reality of resurrection is unknown should not be misunderstood. It is completely unknown in the sense that we have no direct experience of it and therefore no resources out of which we can picture or imagine it literally. But it is not unknown in the sense that there is nothing we can say about it. Otherwise we would not know how to apply the metaphor of 'awakening' to it. We would not know what would count as evidence for or against the truth of our statements about it.

By using the words 'completely unknown' in this context Pannenberg has left himself open to misunderstanding. But what he has written in other contexts clearly excludes such misunderstanding.[4] At least the defining characteristics are known from the context of apocalyptic expectation in which it arises. Resurrection is entry into salvation. It is therefore enlargement and enhance-

---

[2] I think this is fair. There are passages in late Jewish apocalyptic which, quoted out of context, give the impression that what they have in mind is a crude reconstitution of the person exactly as he was before death. But when one considers that almost everything else about apocalyptic is symbolic there are really no grounds for taking such images literally. Certainly St Paul did not (see 1 Cor. 15: 35–56).

[3] Pannenberg, *Jesus—God and Man*, p. 74 (my italics).

[4] Especially in 'Dogmatische Erwägungen zur Auferstehung Jesu', *Kerygma und Dogma* (1968), No. 14, Vol. 2, p. 105 ff.

ment rather than diminution of life. For statements about the resurrection to have definite meaning we do not need to know what form this enhancement will take. We need only entertain the expectation that it will be recognizable as such when we enter upon it. It is in this sense that the metaphor of awakening applies. It is total transformation (cf. 1 Cor. 15 : 35 ff.); yet recognizable identity is preserved. It is fulfilment of hope and man's openness beyond the world. It is participation in the eternity of God and in his future rule in the Kingdom proclaimed by Jesus. The promise of it raises expectations which will either be fulfilled or remain unfulfilled. The truth or falsehood of the assertions about resurrection in the apocalyptic tradition rest ultimately upon this. It is important to make this clear in order to safeguard Pannenberg's statements about the symbolic character of the concept of resurrection from the charge (applicable to some other modern, symbolic interpretations) that it voids the doctrine of truth conditions and so of assertive meaning.

Secondly, subject to that safeguard, Pannenberg's emphasis on the symbolic character of apocalyptic imagery generally and of the concept of resurrection in particular has important apologetic significance for the presentation of the Christian tradition to the modern world. The unacceptability of the apocalyptic tradition in the modern world is due largely to the fact that it is foreign to the style of our imaginations. But the essential point about apocalyptic is not its imagery as such. That is something characteristic of a particular time and place in the history of religions. The apocalyptic tradition has played a crucial part in disclosing to mankind that infinite openness beyond the world which is man's distinctive and identifying characteristic. Thus, as well as being a local phenomenon of late Judaism, apocalyptic corresponds to something universally human. Therefore its essential meaning is foreign to no culture.[5] To live as a being

[5] This interpretation of the universal validity of apocalyptic must be distinguished from attempts such as that of Bultmann to separate the universally valid meaning of apocalyptic from its form, e.g. by translating it into terms of existentialist philosophy. In Pannenberg's view, the meaning cannot be separated from the expectation of the end of history as a future event.

open beyond the world one must hope beyond the world. The form of apocalyptic thought thus corresponds to the true form of human existence. This conclusion is anticipated in the apocalyptic vision of Daniel where the consummation of the Kingdom is symbolized by 'one who is in the likeness of a Son of Man', in contrast with the beasts who have preceded him.

Thus to receive the Christian message it is necessary to stand within the apocalyptic frame of thought at least to the extent of recognizing its universal validity.

'But can the apocalyptic conceptual world still be binding for us? In any case, one cannot deny this question without being clear about its importance. Although the apocalyptic concept of the end of the world may be untenable in many details, its fundamental elements, the expectation of a resurrection of the dead in connection with the end of the world and the Final Judgment can still remain true even for us. At any rate the primitive Christian motivation for faith in Jesus as the Christ of God, in his exaltation, in his identification with the Son of Man, is essentially bound to the apocalyptic expectation for the end of history to such an extent that one must say that if the apocalyptic expectation should be totally excluded from the possibility for us, then the early Christian faith in Christ is also excluded; then, however, the continuity would be broken between that which might still remain as Christianity after such a reduction and Jesus himself, together with the primitive Christian proclamation through Paul's time. One must be clear about the fact that when one discusses the truth of the apocalyptic expectation of a future judgment and a resurrection of the dead, one is dealing directly with the basis of the Christian faith. Why the man Jesus can be the ultimate revelation of God, why in him God is supposed to have appeared, remains incomprehensible apart from the horizon of the apocalyptic expectation.' [6]

[6] *Jesus—God and Man*, pp. 82–3.

Knowledge of Jesus obtained within the pattern of apocalyptic thought may be expressed in terms of other patterns of thought—as for example in Greek *logos* christology. But it cannot be initiated within these other patterns; for apocalyptic belongs to the Christ-event itself as its context and therefore as the form in which its meaning is inherent in the event.

JESUS' RESURRECTION AS AN HISTORICAL PROBLEM

We should be in a position to approach this problem free of the assumption that 'the dead do not rise'.

There are two immediately apparent facts from which we can begin. (a) The resurrection stories have been handed down to us in the tradition of the Scriptures. (b) In the very earliest strata of that tradition, in so far as these can be distinguished and uncovered by source-criticism, the resurrection of Jesus is presented as the decisive ground for faith.

Many attempts have been made to reverse this relation and to account for the resurrection stories as the product of the faith of the early church (Bultmann). Pannenberg rejects this suggestion on historical grounds. There is clear evidence, he claims, that after the crucifixion of Jesus the disciples left Jerusalem in despair. There is no way of explaining the rise of faith apart from some further event which initiated it. Therefore a critical historical approach forces us to acknowledge that some objective event which was interpreted by the witnesses as the appearance of the resurrected Jesus did take place.

There is some weight in this argument. It has been used by others such as G. Wingren and regarded by them as conclusive. It seems to me, however, that that claims too much for the argument. The capacity of the human mind to generate belief out of its own inner recesses is not to be under-estimated. One therefore needs some additional argument showing why the belief in the resurrection should not be regarded as of subjective origin. But there are such arguments. The first which Pannenberg puts forward rests on the early date of the tradition. It takes time for subjectively generated beliefs to become firmly established as tradition. There seems to have been scarcely enough time for this to have taken place.

The recital of resurrection appearances in 1 Cor. 15 is itself of early date and has already the appearance of a fixed and formalized tradition. This would indicate an earlier origin more or less contemporary with the death of Jesus.

The resurrection appearances of Jesus do have the character of visions. But this does not mean that what was seen was imaginary. To maintain that the appearances were the product of the over-excited imagination of the disciples is inconsistent with the wide distribution of the appearances in space and time. It is too much of a coincidence that similar experiences should have occurred to different people in so many places and at different times. This makes it very improbable that they could be explained in terms of hysterical communication.

I think that in the face of Pannenberg's review of the evidence, if the resurrection were not regarded on *a priori* grounds as an inherently improbable (or impossible) event, then the historical evidence yielded by a rigorously critical use of the documents would be convincing. This is why it is important to think one's way into the apocalyptic pattern of thought. Within that context the resurrection of the dead is not an inherently improbable event, but an *expected* event.

'The expectation of resurrection must already be presupposed as a truth that is given by tradition or anthropologically or is established philosophically when one speaks of Jesus' resurrection.' [7]

This evidence does not establish the actuality of the resurrection of Jesus beyond all doubt. But, considered in the light of the expectations inherent in its own context, it does provide ground for reasonable belief and so for faith as hopeful trust in the promises of God.

[7] *Ibid.*, p. 81.

Pannenberg also argues for the reality of the empty tomb. This is a much more difficult undertaking and the arguments are less convincing. For example, he has to account for the fact that St Paul does not so much as mention it. His contention that this is simply because it never happened to be relevant to any of Paul's arguments is hardly an adequate explanation of this omission. But he is aware that the case here is much weaker and rightly emphasizes that the crucial evidence is the resurrection appearances of Jesus and that the validity of that tradition is wholly independent of the empty tomb.

THE RESURRECTION AND THE DIVINITY OF JESUS

Many attempts have been made in the past to trace the doctrine of the divinity of the Christ back to the earthly life of Jesus. This has been difficult in view of the known tendency of the early church to read its own theology back into the pre-Easter life and teaching of Jesus and to put its own theology into his mouth. This means that every claim to divine status ascribed to Jesus must be suspect. Moreover, it is difficult to reconcile such an open claim with true human consciousness.

In view of such difficulties, others like Bultmann have attempted to find the source of the doctrine of the person of Christ in the faith of the early church. But, for reasons stated above, it is difficult to think of faith and its content arising by spontaneous generation.

Pannenberg's suggestion that the belief in the divinity of Christ is to be traced directly to the resurrection is more plausible than either of these. It adequately explains the rise of the belief in the divinity of Jesus and why that belief should have coloured so heavily the reporting of his earthly life. It has the added attraction that it leaves open the possibility that Jesus had (in this particular sense) divine status and yet in his earthly life experienced the limitations essential to human consciousness. If this position can stand critical examination, then it solves many of the perennial problems and contradictions of christology.

Pannenberg's argument (as is so often the case) looks speciously simple. In fact it is both complex and subtle. To approach it, one should recall what has been said above about revelation as history. Revelation is understood as the self-revelation of God. This revelation is indirect. God is disclosed through his action in history. But God cannot be fully disclosed in history until the end of history, for the future is always open and further radical novelty is always possible. Apocalyptic arrives at the notion of the totality and the completion of history. In that completion or end of history, the Glory of God will be fully revealed. That end or completion of history includes the general resurrection of the dead. This is the only context in which Jewish tradition considers resurrection. Therefore when Jesus rises from the dead there is no option but to treat this event as a foretaste of the end. Therefore the self-disclosure of God is complete in Jesus Christ, risen and glorified.

But where self-disclosure is complete it must be a once-for-all event. Any further disclosure would imply the incompleteness of the former disclosure. Therefore the event must be unique.

Furthermore, where self-disclosure is complete there must be real identity of the person disclosed and the disclosing medium. Otherwise the medium would obscure the self-disclosure to some extent and the disclosure would not be complete. Therefore there must be a real identity of God and the risen Christ. Thus the doctrine of the incarnation derives from and is dependent on the recognition of Jesus as the final revelation of God. This derives from an acknowledgement of the reality of his resurrection as historic event and recognition of the meaning of that event within its apocalyptic context. This order of knowing cannot be reversed.

Granted for the moment then that this is the order of knowing (*ordo cognoscendi*), what of the order of being (*ordo essendi*)? That is to say, granted that it is in the resurrection that Jesus is *recognized* as the Christ who is one with God, is that also the moment in which he *becomes* the Christ of God? There are passages, especially in the earliest strata of the New Testament tradition, which might suggest an affirmative answer. Romans 1:3–4 is particularly significant in this connection:

> 'Concerning his Son Jesus Christ our Lord, who was made of the seed of David according to the flesh and marked off [ὁρισθέντος] as the son of God with power, according to the spirit of holiness by the resurrection from the dead.'

Pannenberg, to his great credit does not try to impose on the New Testament a unity of opinion which manifestly is not there. The relation of Jesus to God is variously conceived in the New Testament and these different conceptions relate to different aspects of his life. Thus it can appear to be implied that Jesus became (was adopted as) the Son of God at his resurrection, his baptism, his birth, or any other significant moment in his life. But without doubt his resurrection was recognized as the crucial step in the disclosure of his relation to the Father. But 'the resurrection has retroactive force for Jesus' pre-Easter activity'. [8] Therefore it would not be true to say that Jesus did not become the Son of God until his resurrection.

This is a sentence of enormous importance and monstrous difficulty. Pannenberg is sympathetic to the symbol of adoption as it appears in the New Testament. 'Nevertheless', he says:

> 'the idea that Jesus had received divinity only as a consequence of his resurrection is not tenable. We have seen in our discussion of the meaning of the resurrection event that the character of the confirmation of Jesus' pre-Easter claim is connected with the resurrection. To this extent the resurrection event has retroactive power. Jesus did not simply become something that he previously had not been, but his pre-Easter claim was confirmed by God. This confirmation, the manifestation of Jesus' "divine Sonship" by God, is the new thing brought by the Easter event. However, as confirmation, the resurrection has retroactive force for Jesus' pre-Easter activity, which taken by itself was not yet recognizable as being divinely authorized

[8] *Ibid.*, p. 135.

and its authorization was also not yet definitively settled. However, this has been revealed in its divine legitimation in the light of Jesus' resurrection.

The idea that an event has retroactive force is familiar from legal terminology. Ordinances or laws can be said to have retroactive force. Such a conception is foreign, however, to the usual ontological thought. Nevertheless, what is said above does not involve something unique about the Christ event that would be ontologically incomprehensible and thus reduced to an empty assertion, but it involves a matter of universal ontological relevance. To be sure, for the concept of essence in the Greek philosophical tradition this aspect remained hidden, because for Greek thought everything has always been in its essence what it is. However, for thought that does not proceed from a concept of essence that transcends time, for which the essence of a thing is not what persists in the succession of change, for which, rather, the future is open in the sense that it will bring unpredictably new things that nothing can resist as absolutely unchangeable—for such thought only the future decides what something is. Then the essence of a man, of a situation, or even of the world in general is not yet to be perceived from what is now visible. Only the future will decide it. It is still to be shown what will become of man and of the world's situation in the future. To that extent it is not a special case that Jesus' essence is established retroactively from the perspective of the end of his life, from his resurrection, not only for our knowledge but in its being. Had Jesus not been raised from the dead, it would have been decided that he also had not been one with God previously. But through his resurrection it is decided, not only so far as our knowledge is concerned, but with respect to reality, that Jesus is one with God and retroactively that he was also already one with God previously.' [9]

It is characteristic of Pannenberg that he should thus set out

[9] *Ibid.*, pp. 135–6.

an almost wholly novel system of ontology in a couple of paragraphs. It is very difficult to know exactly what he is proposing and how to test its credibility. The view that a being is essentially what it will become is not strange or unfamiliar. It has familiar roots in Greek philosophy. It can be illustrated by examples such as the acorn which can reasonably be said to contain the essence of the oak tree. But this familiar sense, in which a thing may be said to be in essence what it will become, is explicitly excluded by Pannenberg.

In rejecting this as a model of the mode of the divine being of the Christ in his earthly history he is surely right. Even though the New Testament does speak of Jesus growing in favour with God and man, there is no suggestion that his divinity is a potentiality developing within his humanity.

What, then, does it mean to say that the Resurrection of Christ has retroactive significance for his pre-Easter life? The legal analogy which is offered in the passage quoted above is not really very helpful. It is true that laws sometimes do have retroactive significance. Apart from the fact that this would generally be regarded by jurists as bad legal practice, such legislation operates by fiat or decree. It can determine legal status, but not ontological status. For example, a state may legislate that the humanity of black people is different and separate from the humanity of white people. But mercifully that does not alter the facts. It does not determine the essential humanity of either.

One could perhaps argue that in this case the decree is a divine decree. A divine decree, unlike a human decree, has creative power. Therefore it can determine ontological status retroactively. There is, perhaps, an element of the truth in this if one relates it to the notion of election and God's eternal decree. (I shall attempt to relate Pannenberg's ontology of the person of Christ to his doctrine of God's eternity presently.) But stated thus baldly, it implies an extraneous supernaturalism which would be out of sympathy with the New Testament and Pannenberg's own thought. Besides, the point is one of general ontology. He is not pleading a special ontology for the Christ-event.

There are several things that can be said in explanation and defence of Pannenberg's view of the retroactive force of the resurrection. The first is a linguistic point. There are some attributes which apply to a person in the whole of his extended identity in time. If I were to say, 'Scotland's best-known poet was born on 25 January, 1759' it would be both foolish and perverse for someone to reply 'That cannot be true, for at that date he still had not written any poetry'. We would not argue with such a man. If we took him seriously at all we would explain that he had misunderstood the 'grammar' of that kind of attribute. Such an attribute applies to a man in the whole of his identity.

The attribute of being the Christ is *par excellence* an attribute of this kind. Talk of someone *becoming* the Christ is a contradiction in terms. Pannenberg sees this quite clearly. 'The light that falls back on the pre-Easter Jesus from the resurrection involves his person as a whole.' [10]

Secondly, it must be kept in mind that the question about Jesus' status as the Christ is a question about his eternal relation to God. Pannenberg's doctrine of the relation of time and eternity is of cogent relevance here. According to this there is a sense in which the whole of time is compresent to God. God has a real life in time, but not as we experience time. Time is never a limitation upon God. He is not excluded from the past or the future as we are. In the final manifestation of the truth of God Jesus' resurrection will be compresent with his birth. In his resurrection as well as in his birth it is in anticipation of this end-time that he is the Christ. It is Jesus' relation to God that makes him the Christ, not his relation to us. Therefore it is in the divine perspective on time that the relation between Jesus pre-Easter and his post-Easter existence is to be understood.

Thirdly, we have to free ourselves from the persistent influence of Greek—particularly Platonic—metaphysics if we are to appreciate Pannenberg's point. In a footnote associated with the

[10] *Ibid.*, p. 141.

passage quoted above he refers to his article 'What is Truth?'[11] There he makes two points which have a bearing on the retroactive significance of the resurrection. Firstly, he sharpens the distinction between the Greek and the Hebrew view of truth. For the Greeks truth is something hidden under the changing appearance of things. For the Hebrews the truth is something which happens. For the first way of thinking an event in time cannot have constitutive force for the eternal essence of a thing. For the second way of thinking it can. If the Hebraic habit of mind has superior validity (Pannenberg believes he can show that it has), then it makes sense to say that the resurrection of Jesus has constitutive force for the whole course of his existence in time.

In the same article he argues that truth, in so far as it is available to us within history is always relative to and limited by the finite horizon of our standpoint. Only at the end of history is the truth of all that has happened finally established. Jesus in his resurrection is the anticipation of that end of history. His resurrection, therefore, has constitutive force for the truth of what may be said not only of his own pre-Easter history but of every event in history.

These considerations by no means remove all the difficulties and obscurities surrounding Pannenberg's doctrine of the christological significance of the resurrection. But they do make it more plausible.

I said above that it is typical of Pannenberg that he should try to present an entirely new ontology in a couple of paragraphs. In the strict sense of the terms this is true. His historical habit of mind makes him disinclined to dwell on explicitly metaphysical themes. He prefers to let the novelty of his metaphysical conceptions disclose itself indirectly in the categorical structure of his more concrete talk about history and the world. If one bears this in mind, then his exposition of the ontological significance of the resurrection for the historic life of Jesus is not just the few

---

[11] Pannenberg, *Basic Questions in Theology*, Vol. II, pp. 1–27.

paragraphs in which he deals with it explicitly. It is the implicit content of almost everything he has written.

He himself is fully aware of the unsolved problems and difficulties surrounding his suggestions for a new approach to christology. In the introduction to *Jesus—God and Man* he says:

'To be sure, I am far from supposing that the central problem would be sufficiently clarified by that [the approach of the theology of history]. Rather, the Christological discussions in this book point at every step to ontological and epistemological implications that need their own comprehensive discussion.' [12]

Pannenberg's primary contribution is in the discovery of a new theological method. Therefore a good deal of his work is essentially programmatic. He sketches out new solutions to major problems. The work of elaborating and testing these solutions in detail remains to be done. Because of the way in which he has married historico-critical to systematic methods, it is likely that this will be carried forward by teams of scholars rather than by individuals, in the manner exemplified in his *Revelation as History*, where he co-operates with scholars from various disciplines.

It is as a programme of work still to be done that his suggestions about the christological significance of the resurrection of Jesus are of primary importance.

As well as presenting obscurities and difficulties, these suggestions offer some very attractive possibilities. In particular, Pannenberg's account of the divinity of Jesus successfully avoids the monstrous suggestion of a God–man hybrid walking about on the face of the earth. It allows Jesus to be, in his subjective experience, wholly and simply man during the period between his birth and his death. Yet objectively and in truth—in that truth which will be disclosed only at the end of history—it lets him be also the presence of God within history.

[12] p. 12. Some of these problems receive rather fuller discussion in *Theology and the Kingdom of God.*

This is an interesting and important new attempt to satisfy the very exacting requirements of the creed of Chalcedon—to unite God and man in Christ in such a way that God remains God and man remains man; to keep them distinct without dividing the identity of the person.

> 'Viewed from the confirmation of Jesus' claim by his resurrection, the inner logic of the matter dictates that Jesus was always one with God, not just after a certain date in his life. And in view of God's eternity, the revelatory character of Jesus' resurrection means that God was always one with Jesus, even before his earthly birth. Jesus is from all eternity the representative of God in creation. Were it otherwise, Jesus would not be in person the one revelation of the eternal God. We can no longer think of God in his eternal deity without Jesus. That is indeed, the meaning of Jesus' resurrection.' [13]

Far from wishing to suggest that there was a time when Jesus was not the eternal Son of God, Pannenberg feels some uneasiness with the traditional incarnational theology because it suggests that there was a time when the eternal Son of God was independent of and separate from the man Jesus. This, he suggests, exhibits a misunderstanding of the relation between time and eternity. It betrays a mythological understanding of the action of God within the world. It separates the two elements which should be distinguished without separation—the eternal Son of God and the man Jesus.[14]

The incarnational mode of speech about Jesus is not illegitimate so long as it maintains its connection with the Old Testament view of history and the relation between time and eternity. But once let it become dissociated from that and it becomes sheer mythology about the 'descent' of a god.

Before we can take Pannenberg's view of the relation between God and man in Jesus Christ any further, we have to go fairly carefully into his doctrine of God.

[13] *Jesus—God and Man*, p. 153.
[14] Cf. *Ibid.*, pp. 134 ff.

Chapter 6

JEWS, GREEKS AND GOD

We shall approach Pannenberg's doctrine of God in two stages; firstly, with reference to the philosophical doctrine of God; secondly, with reference to the doctrine of God's trinity in unity. The philosophical doctrine of God presents special problems for Pannenberg. He stresses the apocalyptic element in Christianity. On his interpretation of the faith it must remain at the centre. It is the key without which nothing in the Gospel would make sense. The meaning of the life, death and resurrection of Jesus as the ultimate self-disclosure of God is inseparably bound to this traditio-historical expression of the peculiarly Jewish view of history as God's history.

But it was this apocalyptic element which was a laughing-stock to the Greeks. It appeared to be completely incompatible with the spirit of their philosophy. They could hardly begin to take it seriously. The idea of a God who involves himself in history was incredible to them. The idea of the resurrection of the body was not a serious candidate for philosophical investigation. The recognition of an element of unpredictable contingency in the divine will—and so at the heart of reality—was to them sheer irrationalism.

Thorough investigation of the situation which this created—especially for the doctrine of God—in the Hellenistic church is not a mere matter of theological archeology. It is a problem which remained largely unsolved and is, Pannenberg believes, the root of much contemporary atheism.

Why let the problem of the application of Greek philosophical concepts to the doctrine of God complicate the problem? Why not, with Tertullian, attempt to remain wholly within the orbit of biblical concepts?

One sometimes gets the impression that Pannenberg would like to do just this. He is much more at home with history and the philosophy of history than he is with metaphysics. But, for one thing, he is much too conscious of the irreversibility of history to attempt such a thing. For better or worse, the fact is that a most unlikely marriage between Hebrew traditio-historical theology and Greek philosophical theology did take place. It had a profound and ineradicable effect on our conceptual grasp of the doctrine of God. That influence is now deeply embedded in our tradition. We cannot now go back upon it and read our Bibles as though we were first-generation Jerusalem Christians to whom none of this had ever happened.

Thus it is in the first instance because of, not in spite of, his historical approach to the question of God that he sees the necessity to accommodate the philosophical approach alongside it.

He refers with some disparagement to those theologies which attempt to go back behind the philosophical and metaphysical elements introduced into the doctrine of God through the encounter with Greek philosophy. In the nineteenth century A. Ritschl lamented the intrusion of theoretical metaphysics into theology as a result of Greek influence. Under Kantian influence, he believed that value judgements rather than theoretical understanding were the proper concern of theology. In the same tradition Harnack regarded Greek metaphysical thought as a corrupting influence on the theology of the living God of the Gospels. A good deal of this anti-metaphysical spirit still persists in modern theology. There are no biblical theologians who remain untouched by it.

The trouble with theologies which divorce faith from knowledge—whether as value judgement, as obedience, as existential decision, as freedom or as commitment—is that they inevitably end up with a god who isn't there. This was illustrated in the evolution of the 'Death of God' theology out of this tradition.

Pannenberg is quite clear that faith derives from knowledge, not the reverse. It therefore rests upon assertions about what is the case. These assertions are of two kinds. First of all there are assertions about particular historical facts—the history of Israel, the life, death and resurrection of Jesus. Secondly, there are assertions about the meaning of these facts in relation to the whole of history. But the 'whole of history' is itself a metaphysical concept which cannot be conceived without reference to what is transcendent and eternal. Therefore we are committed to stating what is the case metaphysically as well as historically. These two types of statement are never wholly unrelated. But they need to be consciously brought into closer relation with one another. You could say that this is what Pannenberg's theological investigations are all about.

Yet to emphasize the apocalyptic context of the Christian message and at the same time uphold and justify the introduction of Greek metaphysical concepts into the tradition requires a stout heart and strenuous thought. It was under the influence of Greek philosophy that the so-called 'metaphysical attributes' of God were systematically developed—his unity, eternity, infinity, changelessness, impassibility, and so on. These doctrines were developed largely in independence from the historical understanding of God in the Old Testament and in the apocalyptic context of the New Testament. They were developed out of the conceptual material already available in the Greek philosophical tradition. Thus God's eternity is conceived as sheer timelessness. He has no positive relation to what is happening in time except as its remote *archē* or originating principle. He is immutable in his being. He is simple and without distinguishable attributes. He is undifferentiated unity. He is impassible and therefore untouched by the world's happenings.

Pannenberg recognizes that these characteristically Greek speculations about the essential nature of the divine cannot be simply rejected out of hand. There is sense in them. They are

88

implied in the ultimacy of God. If God is the ultimate reality, he is eternal. (Whatever can come into existence and go out of existence is part of the world, not its ultimate origin.) Whatever is subject to change cannot be eternal. Whatever can change can cease to be. Whatever is changeless can have no connection with time; for time exists only in relation to change.

In the light of such a development in the doctrine of God, it is not surprising that the apocalyptic context of the message, life and destiny of Jesus was pushed to the periphery of the church's teaching and its historical significance allegorized away.

It is usually said that the delay in the expected return of Christ to bring about the general resurrection of the dead and the final judgement was the reason for the decline of the original apocalyptic message. Pannenberg rejects this explanation. The anticipatory character of the resurrection of Jesus was recognized within the church from the very beginning. Once this is recognized, he points out, the length of the interval between the resurrection of Jesus and the general resurrection which it anticipates does not constitute a serious objection (cf. 1 Cor. 15). It was rather the failure to integrate the thought-forms of apocalyptic theology and Hellenistic philosophy which constituted the real difficulty.

That is little wonder. How can the God of the metaphysical attributes be also the God who actively brings about Israel's history, who discloses his essence in identity with Jesus Christ and who will come at the end of time to gather the world and all its history into his own eternal presence?

Despite their obvious differences, the Judaeo-Christian tradition and Greek philosophy have some decisive elements in common.[1] Firstly, like the biblical tradition, the main stream of Greek philosophy was concerned to discover and enter into appropriate relation with the ultimate origin of all that exists. In

[1] Pannenberg often talks about 'Greek philosophy' as though it were a single tradition. It is mainly Middle Platonism and some elements of Stoic philosophy that he has in mind. He is, understandably in the context, inclined to look at Greek philosophy through the eyes of the early church Fathers, who saw it as a more or less monolithic structure.

this they were not motivated by mere curiosity. They sought salvation by knowledge. They believed that ultimate reality was divine.

The Greek achievement was to discover the universal form of the question which arises out of all finite existence—particularly human existence.

The peculiar destiny of the people of Israel was to receive an answer to this question without fully realizing the universality of its scope.

As we saw above, from about the time of the Exile, Judaism proclaimed that the God of Israel was *also* the God of all nations and the creator of the whole world. But this 'also' plays a tell-tale role. God was thought of in the first instance as the God of Israel. The prophetic proclamation of the universal sovereignty of God was essentially a proclamation about the future—though it had implications for the present. The apocalyptic tradition emphasized the element of futurity still more. In Judaic thought, the gathering-in of the nations was not expected until this future manifestation of the glory of God. Therefore they could, with justification believe that for the time being their concern was with God as the God of Israel.

But as soon as it was believed that the end had already come—even in an anticipatory way—through the message and the resurrection of Jesus, then the practical recognition of the universality of God in his relation to all peoples was immediately demanded.

God had to be proclaimed as the answer to the question about the ultimate origin and destiny of all things wherever men were asking that question. In response to this the mission to the Gentiles was undertaken. Christian theology had to begin to engage in an intellectual bartering of concepts with Hellenistic philosophy. Otherwise Christianity would have remained a cultic sect of Judaism and so been untrue to its own message.

Thus it was *because of*, not in spite of, the apocalyptic character of the message of Jesus that the marriage of apocalyptic proclamation of God and Greek philosophic concepts was proposed. It should, therefore, be possible to consummate that marriage; but not by the sacrifice of one party to the other.

In spite of a remarkable degree of agreement about the transcendence, universality, eternity, unity and spirituality of God these attributes were differently conceived in each tradition. The two traditions could communicate and illuminate one another only through mutual transformation. That mutual transformation has taken place only partially and incompletely. As a result the doctrine of God remains seriously incoherent to this day.

Greek philosophy retained some elements surviving from its roots in Greek religion. The Greek gods were intimately associated with the regularities of nature. Therefore, Pannenberg suggests, Greek thought about the ultimate origin of all things sought an essential and necessary connection between the world and its divine originating principle. This gave rise to the idea of an ultimate divine principle that could be inferred from the order of nature. Within the church this eventually gave rise to the notion of a 'natural theology' wholly independent of the revelation in history. This eventually resulted in a divorce of revealed theology from critical reason. These two paths have different gods at the end of them. To pursue both can only end in confusion. To pursue only one of these paths can only end in error. Revelation divorced from reason cannot represent the universality of God. Reason without revelation cannot know him as the living God—and there is no other. Only if the two are brought together in a new unity can we introduce any coherence into the doctrine of God. But they cannot be brought together just as they are. Without mutual transformation they will not mix. It is contrary to the spirit of honest philosophical doctrine to accept extraneous supplementation from revelation. It is equally contrary to the spirit of revealed theology to admit another area of knowledge of God independent of its disclosures. We can arrive at a coherent doctrine of God only by uniting philosophical and revealed theology in a way that transforms both.

The other contrast of basic importance is that between nature and history. In Greek thought, the ultimate, originating principle discloses its perfection and rationality in the ordered system of the universe. It prevails over disruption and change. In the Hebrew tradition the originator of all things exhibits his originality precisely in bringing about change. He makes all things new. He is the author of the contingency and novelty of history. The fulfilment of his promises surprises his own prophets.

Therefore the Greeks tended to interpret history in the light of nature. The Hebrews tended to interpret nature in the light of history.

This is particularly so in apocalyptic writings where the order of nature is ultimately dependent on what happens contingently and historically. It depends on the faithfulness of God to his promises in history. This is symbolized in the images of the transformation of nature at the end of history. The same thought finds more subtle expression in the Pauline concept of the whole creation groaning and travailing in pain, waiting for the appearing of the sons of God.

It seems to me a pity, however, that Pannenberg sometimes follows the common practice of presenting these contrasts and the tensions to which they give rise within the doctrine of God as the result of tension between the Greek and the Hebrew mind. In my view it should not be presented in ethnic terms. It corresponds to a basic split within human nature.

If we bring together various elements scattered throughout Pannenberg's writings, we can see the problem as a human rather than an ethnic or cultural one. The tension between the philosophical and the historical elements in the Christian doctrine of God correlate with the tension between centredness and openness in humanity. Systematic reason, though open beyond the world, affirms the centredness of stable structures (especially the thinking self) and seeks their ground in ultimate reality. In another context Pannenberg notes the extreme expression of this in the development of Platonism which asserted that ultimate reality is Mind. It even led to the suggestion (which keeps cropping up in philosophy every now and again) that thought creates its own truth.

On the other hand, though centred in the self, historical reason is an expression of our openness. It does not attempt to excogitate the truth. It depends on what is given to it. It has to wait and see what happens. It seeks the truth in what the day brings forth. It looks for meaning in the contingent.

In this way the tensions in our doctrine of God correlate with tensions between our centredness and openness. It is this universal element in the human situation which came to historical expression in the encounter between Jew and Greek in the early church. It is a promise of the Gospel that Jew and Greek will be reconciled in the power of the cross and the resurrection. This involves the reconciliation of the Jew within us all and the Greek within us all.

Remarkably good progress was made in the early church towards the reconciliation by mutual transformation of apocalyptic and philosophical approaches to the doctrine of God. One example which Pannenberg gives of the fruitful outcome of this union is the formulation of the doctrine of creation out of nothing. Neither the traditio-historical theology of Judaism nor the Greek philosophical tradition had been able to achieve this on its own.

But most of the major problems have been left unsolved. We need to think our way back into the apocalyptic framework of thought in order to begin tackling them again.

ETERNITY, IMMUTABILITY AND UNIVERSALITY

There is a particular need to work on these three concepts. Pannenberg's treatment of them—especially his treatment of eternity—is the key to much of his theology.

As already noted, in Greek philosophical tradition God's eternity is implied in his status as the ultimate origin of all existence. Eternity is here interpreted as sheer *atemporality*. It is timelessness. Therefore the knowledge of God is not to be sought in events in time. God is to be known through the contemplation of timeless ideas.

For traditio-historical thinking on the other hand, God is to be known in the memory of past events, in the interest of present events and in the expectation of future events. God's eternity does not consist in his dissociation from time, but in his mastery over time. He is Lord of time as he is Lord of all creation. His eternity is a function of his free sovereignty.[2]

We experience time partly as opportunity, partly as restriction. It is a restriction upon us because we can do nothing about what is past. We can do little about what is to come. The one is 'no more', the other is 'not yet'.

It was noted earlier, in the course of preliminary references to eternity (above, p. 27 ff.), that our own present is something more than the unextended mathematical point between past and future. It has a small but variable extension. So far as anything remains at our disposal it belongs to our present. So Pannenberg believes. Since God is the free, transcendent, omnipotent Lord of creation, there is nothing which is not at his disposal. Therefore everything belongs to his present. He is not timeless. He experiences time (in so far as our concept of 'experience' can be analogically applied to God). But he does not experience time as a restriction excluding him from past or future. For God time must be thought of as pure opportunity. It is occasion for the exercise of his sovereignty and free creativity. This is the basis of Pannenberg's concept, to which reference has already been made, of the compresence of all times to God.

There is a parallel development of the notion of ubiquity in Pannenberg. It does not mean that God is, as it were, evenly distributed through space or obliged by his nature to be wholly present at every point in space. Space is not a restriction to God. It is wholly at his disposal.

But for Pannenberg it is the relation of God to time which is crucial.

These ideas about the relation of God to time are not entirely new. They are to some extent anticipated in classical theism as

---

[2] Pannenberg, *Theology and the Kingdom of God*, pp. 51 ff.

represented for example in St Thomas Aquinas. He taught that the relation of all creatures in time to God is a real relation as far as the creature is concerned; but only a matter of logical relation (*secundum rationem*) as regards God. That is to say, the temporal order of events is preserved in God; but all moments of time cohere for him in an eternal present. This gives ontological priority to the present.

But Pannenberg wants to say something more and something different. He wants to preserve the reality as well as the logical order of time in God. He must do if he is to continue to take history as seriously as he does as the self-disclosure of God. He must do if he is going to treat the promise of the future kingdom of God as a real fulfilment and completion of history and not as an other-worldly imposition upon it.

But how is this to be done without subjecting God to the limiting conditions of time in a way which would deny his eternity, ubiquity and universality and so his divinity?

It is conceded that the Christian Aristotelianism of the late Middle Ages made progress towards a solution. The Aristotelian conception of God as the timeless unmoved mover was partially modified in the light of biblical concepts of the living, active God.[3] But the transformation remained incomplete, 'so that in the Christian scholastics the Aristotelian metaphysics of form remained as an unrecognized and unconquered element.'[4]

To correct this Pannenberg introduces the notion of 'the ontological priority of the future'. This is one of the most important, most original and most difficult concepts in his theology. Yet at one level it is perfectly simple. It can be regarded as a metaphysical transcript of what Jesus was talking about when he proclaimed the future Kingdom of God.

The being of God cannot be conceived apart from his rule. Therefore in so far as his rule in history is something which is 'not yet', 'in a restricted but important sense, God does not yet exist. Since his rule and his being are inseparable, God's being is still in process of coming to be'.[5]

[3] *Ibid.*, p. 139.   [4] *Ibid.*, p. 140.   [5] *Ibid.*, p. 56.

So far the notion of the ontological priority of the future is fairly clear. But when we try to clarify the *restricted sense* in which God's being contains an element of 'not yet' or 'still to come', it becomes increasingly complex. With good reason it has always been held in the Christian tradition that if God lacks some perfection yet to be developed then he is not truly God. Is Pannenberg simply rejecting this axiom?

One naturally thinks in this connection of apparent similarities in the so-called process theology developed by C. Hartshorne and others on the basis of the philosophy of A. N. Whitehead. Whitehead held that, although God in his abstract identity is eternally the same, in his actuality he is in process of change and development concomitant with that of the universe. But Pannenberg, although much of his doctrine of God is in sympathy with the process theologians, explicitly rejects this notion of development in God.

> 'We cannot agree when Whitehead suggests that the futurity of God's kingdom implies a development in God. It is true that from the viewpoint of our finite present, the future is not yet decided. Therefore, the movement of time contributes to deciding what the definite truth is going to be, also with regard to the essence of God. But—and here is the difference from Whitehead—*what turns out to be true in the future will then be evident as having been true all along.*' [6]

This last phrase shows that the 'restricted sense' in which 'God does not yet exist' is very restricted indeed. It can be said only from the relative perspective of our finitude. It does not go beyond the biblical doctrine that in some sense there is a time yet to come when 'God shall be all in all'. (1 Cor. 15:28.)

Many grow impatient with the obscurity of Pannenberg's doctrine of God at this point—especially those who value clarity above insight. I think it must be admitted that all is not clear here. But it must also be recognized that he is here exploring a

---

[6] *Ibid.*, pp. 62 ff. (my italics).

new way of tackling an ancient problem for which no wholly satisfactory and consistent solution has ever been offered—that of God's relation to his creation. If we remove God in impassive sovereignty beyond all interior relation to the world we end with a deistic being very unlike the living God of the Bible. If we bring God unequivocally within the *present* world we end with a pagan divinity. If we think of the *present* world as unequivocally in God, then we deny the independence, contingency and freedom of creation.

What other possibilities are there? Pannenberg has suggested that we should think of the world's relation to God in terms of its future rather than its present. This is a profoundly promising suggestion, for it arises out of biblical, eschatological concepts. If it can be further clarified and elaborated it promises to provide metaphysical accommodation for the living God of the Bible in an age which has lost confidence in its traditional metaphysical categories.

But it does need to be thought through in an exercise at least as elaborate as Whitehead's *Process and Reality*. We need a new philosophy of time. It is possible that when the history of our era comes to be written, it will be seen as the age which struggled to understand time [7] just as the age before it struggled to understand 'being'. But it has become clear that time cannot be understood in abstraction from events. It must be understood in relation to its content as concrete happening. This is the point of contact between Pannenberg's doctrine of revelation as history and his doctrine of the real relation of God to time. The eternity of God is not the closed circle of a timeless present. He is the ground of our freedom and the openness of our future.

With this pointer to a new understanding of God's eternity, a similar operation can be performed on the other metaphysical attributes of God.

Divine immutability is not sheer absence of change or movement. Such a conception of divinity is incompatible with the

[7] E.g. Bergson, Alexander, Einstein, Whitehead, Heidegger, Jaspers, Teilhard de Chardin and many others.

living God of Israel, who judges and repents, who has compassion and redeems, who performs wonders in history. God's immutability is his free sovereignty over events. He is never at the mercy of events. His immutability is also his constancy, his faithfulness.

Similarly, God's unity and simplicity are not an undifferentiated absence of relation and attributes. They are the singleness of his purpose and the certainty of his rule. They will be made manifest in the gathering of all things into himself at the end of time.

Chapter 7

TRINITY IN UNITY

I have already suggested that Pannenberg's view of the relation between time and eternity is the key to most aspects of his theological system. It wholly determines his doctrine of the Trinity. One might perhaps, with more justice, say that it is a view of the relation of time and eternity which arises out of his understanding of the Holy Trinity. It is not a philosophy of time and eternity independently arrived at and subsequently imposed on the doctrine of God. It is an understanding of time which, as Pannenberg sees it, arises directly out of God's self-disclosure in history.

God is eternally Father, Son and Holy Spirit. Yet God is essentially one and indivisible; for whatever is composite can disintegrate. Whatever can disintegrate can cease to be. Whatever can cease to be is not God.

If one thinks within the context of the apocalyptic expectation, the resurrection of Jesus establishes that he is the final and complete revelation of God—of the one universal, eternal, indivisible God. But Jesus also experienced his own identity over against the Father. He prayed to God as his Father. He trusted him, loved him, adored him, obeyed him. Even if Jesus never actually thought of himself as 'Son of God'—even if the application of that title to Jesus is entirely the invention of post-Easter christology—there can be little doubt that Jesus did experience a peculiarly intimate filial relation to God.

If there is identity of essence between Jesus and God, then

99

this experience of the faithful and obedient child of God belongs to the eternal essence of God.

Can one infer directly from the religious experience of Jesus (whatever one takes it to be) to the essential and interior mystery of the being of God? Whatever may be the initial improbabilities surrounding this suggestion, there is a kind of imperious logic behind Pannenberg's position. It forces the objector to be quite clear about the point at which he lays down the gauntlet.

The objector must submit to being catechized. Does the objector deny that Jesus rose from the dead? In that case the debate is not concerned with the doctrine of the Trinity. It is a question of history which must be dealt with in a different way. The question of the tri-unity of God arises only for those who believe in the resurrection of Jesus.

If it is admitted that Jesus did rise from the dead, then it must be asked: What does this mean? Within the apocalyptic context it means that this is a preview of the end of history and the end of time. As such it is a disclosure of the one true God whose essence is finally revealed only at the end of history. Therefore the experience of the distinction between himself and God, which belongs to the earthly life of Jesus Christ, belongs to the inner life of God.

It seems to me that there are really only two points at which one can resist the logic of this argument.

One can deny the actuality of the resurrection of Jesus. In that case Pannenberg would defend his position on straightforward historico-critical grounds. The question at issue would then be of the same order as deciding, let us say, whether Joan of Arc was burned at the stake and what the significance of that event amounted to.

Or, one can deny the validity of the apocalyptic context in which the event is interpreted and assessed. But this is not really a serious alternative. If the apocalyptic context of the event is bogus and Jesus really did rise from the dead, then there is no way left to make sense of such an extraordinary occurrence.

If one grants the reality of the resurrection then there is no alternative but to admit identity of essence between Jesus and

God. In that case it is difficult to deny that this experience of the faithful child of God belongs to the eternal essence of God. This means that the eternal essence of God is revealed in the terrible and marvellous events which took place at the time of the death and resurrection of Jesus.

If there is identity of essence between Jesus and God, then this experience of the obedient and faithful child of God belongs to the eternal essence of God. It is the eternity of God that is revealed in the anticipation of the end of time in Jesus Christ. Therefore the distinction that Jesus experienced between himself and the Father belongs eternally to God.

> 'God's essence as it is revealed in the Christ-event thus contains within itself the twofoldness, the tension and the relation of Father and Son. The deity of Jesus cannot therefore have the sense of undifferentiated identity with the divine nature, as if in Jesus God the Father himself had appeared in human form and suffered on the cross . . . The differentiation of Father and Son in God himself must be maintained, because this differentiation, which is characteristic of the relation of the historical Jesus to God, must be characteristic of the essence of God himself if Jesus as a person is God's revelation.' [1]

This is an extremely subtle and difficult argument. As theologians go, Pannenberg has a relatively simple style, and an unpretentious way of presenting his suggestions. This can often give the impression that something simple and naïvely biblicist— almost fundamentalist—is being said. Such an impression is wholly mistaken.

The above argument is something of a logical *tour de force*. It attempts to prove the differentiation of the Son from the Father from the identity of the Son with the Father. In a curious way it succeeds. If Jesus is divine and God is one, then we must find room in our conception of God for the experience of Jesus. The argument succeeds, but it creates an enormous number of logical

---

[1] Pannenberg, *Jesus—God and Man*, pp. 159 ff.

and metaphysical problems which have still to be solved. Perhaps one should say that it unearths problems which have been there all the time.

We have been able to avoid many conceptual and metaphysical problems connected with the doctrine of the Trinity and christology simply because, for almost two millennia, we have been willing to talk two largely unrelated languages about God. (I refer to the traditions of Hebrew and Greek conceptuality discussed in the previous chapter.) When one finds that Pannenberg raises more problems than he solves for theology—and indeed he does—one should not complain. If a man creates problems that are unreal, then by all means complain. But if he brings to light problems which have been there all the time, he is an honest workman.

What is Pannenberg really saying about the relation of the Son to the Father in the above argument? It is not just a clever piece of logical sleight-of-hand. Basically it is an expression of the Christian contention that our interpretation of the concept 'God' must be determined by our understanding of the history and life of Jesus. We should not impose upon the life and destiny of Jesus an interpretation derived from a non-eschatological preconception about the nature of God.

Pannenberg's approach to the doctrine of God has extremely important apologetic significance in the modern world. As has already been remarked, modern man begins with a conviction about the humanity of Jesus. If he is to arrive at a Christian understanding of God it is from there that he must set out.

In Pannenberg's account of the relation of the persons within the Godhead, the second person of the Trinity is not some essence or metaphysical entity other than Jesus of Nazareth. The eternal communion within the Godhead between the Father and the Son is not some ghostly, metaphysical transaction. It is precisely what took place between them in the birth, life, death and resurrection of Jesus of Nazareth. In the compresence of all times in the end-time of God Jesus belongs to the eternity of God because he is the one in whom that end-time comes about.

It is not easy, however, to drive this attractive suggestion of Pannenberg's all the way home to a clear intellectual appreciation. What is the relation between the identity and the differentiation of the Son and the Father? What is its ontological *significance*?

Pannenberg is quite explicit in stating that he regards the identity of God the Father with Jesus as an identity of essence. But the differentiation between them belongs to the essence. I can only take this to mean that the Father and the Son share a common essence in two separate identities. This is perfectly orthodox. It is precisely what the church has been saying ever since the council of Chalcedon in 451. The relation of the Father and the Son is there described as the sharing of one *ousia* (essence) by two *hypostaseis* (identities).[2]

But it is clear that Pannenberg wants to press on beyond Chalcedon to a less formal and more vivid understanding of the relation between the Father and the Son. He wants to show us from the Son what can be known of the life of the living God. And so without altogether renouncing the Greek conceptuality in which the doctrine of the Trinity is traditionally expressed he is fully conscious that ultimately one cannot express an eschatological doctrine of God in terms of non-eschatological metaphysics.

In Greek philosophical tradition, the truth is something lying behind the flux of events which needs to be uncovered.

In the Hebrew eschatological tradition, the truth is something which happens. In particular it is what happens at the end of time when the whole history of every creature is disclosed. This determines essence and identity. Therefore 'essence' and 'identity' have to be transformed into eschatological concepts if they are adequately to describe God's trinity in unity.

The same tension appears within the concept of *logos* or divine Word when it is used to describe the second person in the Trinity. Pannenberg recognizes its advantages as a genuine clarification. It offered a way of making Jesus' unity with the Father and at the same time his differentiation from the Father

---

[2] The sense of *hypostasis* in Chalcedon is 'a subject in which attributes or a nature can inhere'—i.e. an individual identity.

understandable. It did so in a way which was universally comprehensible through the whole of the Hellenistic world. It also gave expression to the involvement of the Son in the creation of the world.

But, Pannenberg warns us, unless this conception is wholly transformed by being integrated into the apocalyptic framework of Christian belief, then it interprets the second person of the Trinity in a seriously distorted way. Firstly, if *logos* is understood in Platonic-Stoic terms, he must be subordinate to the one God, the Father Almighty, simply because he is begotten by the Father. Interpreted in a Greek context, this tends to drive a wedge between the eternal Son of God, the pre-existent Christ, and the man Jesus of Nazareth. It gives rise to the suggestion that the eternal communion between the Father and the Son, the *logos*, is something different from the personal relation between the man Jesus and the heavenly Father whom he trusted and obeyed. This opens the way for talk of what I have already referred to as a 'ghostly metaphysical transaction' between the Father and the Son in a timeless eternity—a communion which seems to have very little to do with what went on between Jesus and his heavenly Father. Pannenberg comments with justifiable surprise on the way in which the Apologists and many of the Fathers who took up the *logos* concept were able to speak of the eternal relation between the Father and the Son with scarcely any reference to the actual history of Jesus.

Pannenberg seems to want to say that the eternal relationship between the Father and the Son *is* what happened between Jesus and God in the Gospel story. This is brought into the heart of God through the resurrection and the relation of the resurrection to the end of time in which all time is gathered up. (But the issues raised here also involve questions about the interpretation of the doctrine of the two 'natures' in Christ and they will be referred to again in that context.)

This understanding of eternal divine Sonship is closely related to Pannenberg's understanding of the role of the *logos* or divine Word in creation:

'In the beginning was the Word, and the Word was with God, and the Word was God. He was in the beginning with God; all things were made through him, and without him was not anything made that was made.' (John 1:1–3.)

The difficulty of Pannenberg's suggestions about this lie partly in their novelty and originality. He says:

'The statement that all things and beings are created through Jesus Christ means that the *eschaton* that has appeared beforehand in Jesus represents the time and point from which the creation took place. According to the Biblical understanding, the essence of things will be decided only in the future. What they are is decided by what they will become. Thus the creation happens from the end, from the ultimate future.'[3]

This is very difficult and bears a lot of thinking about. In a final chapter of *Jesus—God and Man*, he further elucidates his position:

'On the basis of the eschatologically oriented Israelite understanding of truth, according to which the essence of a thing has not always existed—even though hiddenly—but is decided only by what becomes of it, the predestination of all things toward Jesus, their eschatological summation through Jesus, is identical with their creation through Jesus. Every creature receives through him as the eschatological judge its ultimate illumination, its ultimate place, its ultimate definition in the context of the whole creation. The essence of all events and figures is to be ultimately defined in the light of him because their essence is decided on the basis of their orientation to him. To that extent, creation of all things is mediated through Jesus. Christ's mediation of creation is not to be thought of primarily in terms of the temporal beginning of the world. It is rather to be understood in terms of the whole of the world process that receives its unity and meaning in the light of its end that has

[3] *Jesus—God and Man*, p. 169.

appeared in advance in the history of Jesus, so that the essence of every individual occurrence, whose meaning is relative to the whole to which it belongs, is first decided in the light of this end. To be sure, the cosmos with which we are familiar can be supposed to have a temporal beginning, but to speak of the creation of the world does not refer just to this beginning but to the world process as a whole. This is conceivable, because the creation must be understood as an act of God's eternity, even though what is created by this eternal act has a temporal beginning and a temporal becoming. However, God's eternal act of creation will be entirely unfolded in time first in the *eschaton*. Only at the *eschaton* will what is created out of God's eternity be consummated in the accomplishment of its own temporal becoming. Thus, the temporal unfolding of the divine act of creation is to be understood from the perspective of its eschatological fulfilment, not from the perspective of the beginning of the world. Certainly the beginning of the world is to be conceived as established by God, not, however, taken by itself in isolation but seen with the totality of the world from the perspective of its end. If the *eschaton* toward which all things have their being has already appeared in an anticipatory way in Jesus, he is, as the one exalted to be the eschatological Judge, also the one from whom all things come. Only from him, through him, do all things have their essential nature (1 Cor. 8:6).'[4]

THE HOLY SPIRIT

Pannenberg is on easier ground when he emphasizes the essentially eschatological character of the Holy Spirit. This is something that has been fairly well understood ever since the revival of biblical theology in the early days of the 'dialectical theology' movement. But it has not always been so and one cannot count on such understanding even today. The tendency of the Romantic

[4] *Ibid.*, pp. 391–2.

movement to think of the Spirit only as the agent in inspiration or of scholasticism to think of him as an essential adjunct to the process of revelation, conceived in isolation from the apocalyptic context of the Gospel, still persists.

With full backing from modern biblical scholarship, Pannenberg stresses that in the prophetic tradition of Israel the outpouring of the Spirit of God on all flesh was to be a central feature of the final fulfilment of the promises of God and the vindication of his divinity at the end of time.

But within the Old Testament, the Spirit was not primarily a source of supernatural enlightenment (as he came to be in some strands of Christian tradition). He was the spirit of life in the broadest sense. This meant biological life as well as what we would now call spiritual life. Post-Exilic Judaism tended to associate a definitive outpouring of the Spirit with the coming of the Lord's Anointed. It was believed that the Spirit is given to men now by measure and according to need and circumstance. In the end-time the Spirit would rest wholly and eternally upon men.

Whether this association of biological as well as spiritual life with the Spirit of God can again become a working concept in the modern world is a question which Pannenberg raises, but does not fully answer.[5] One could wish that he had devoted more of his very considerable hermeneutical skill to this problem. The matter is urgent in view of the new ecological crisis of the whole of humanity. Our relation to the entire biosphere has become a matter of crisis. The time is overdue for a recovery of the Old Testament understanding of the Spirit.

But Pannenberg sees quite clearly that we cannot simply resuscitate the ancient Israelite understanding of biological life. Modern biochemistry has made that impossible. Neither can we make a direct assault on the problem in restoring the 'spiritual' view of nature developed in the Romantic movement. However one might admire it in its better representatives, that too is culturally *passé*.

---

[5] But see Pannenberg, *Spirit, Faith and Church*, pp. 13 ff.

Despite the urgency of the problem, I am sure Pannenberg is absolutely right in holding that before it can be tackled there is a much more fundamental theological job of work that needs to be done. We need a clearer understanding of the relation of the Spirit to Jesus, to his resurrection, to the end-time which that event anticipates, and so to God the Father who is finally revealed therein.

As the Spirit who will be poured out on all flesh in the end-time the Holy Spirit is the Spirit of the resurrection. This is central to the apocalyptic context of Jesus' life and destiny. This is where we must begin. It is by the power of the Holy Spirit that Jesus is risen from the dead. This is what fundamentally determines the sense in which he is the Spirit of life. It is the relation of men to Jesus that determines their status and condition in the final resurrection. Therefore everything that stands in relation to the resurrected Lord is filled with the new power of the life of the divine Spirit. The Spirit incorporates men into the world-wide body of Christ.

The Spirit is the Spirit of God, for it is God who raises the dead. God the Father gives life by uniting to himself. 'For as the Father has life in himself, so he has granted the Son also to have life in himself.' Therefore it is the Holy Spirit who unites the Father and the Son. Thus all who receive life in the Son receive it by being united to him in the Holy Spirit. So the Holy Spirit is the Spirit of the Son. He is also the Spirit indwelling in the community of those who believe the message of the resurrection with faith.

What is all this about, and how, if the Spirit is all these things, is it possible to speak of the Spirit as a third identity (*hypostasis*) or person (*prosōpon, persona*) within the unity of God?

It is all the harder for Pannenberg to establish the distinct identity of the Spirit since he insists that illumination by the Spirit is not another event alongside the hearing of the message of Jesus Christ. He is received in and with the message. The outpouring of the Spirit is not another event alongside the final revelation of God in Jesus Christ.

Pannenberg's argument for the distinct personality of the Spirit is in essentially the same form as his argument for the distinction between Father and Son. He derives the distinction from the unity. The distinction is experienced as an element within the unity. Jesus receives and experiences his unity with God as unity with the Spirit of God. We experience our unity with the Christ (which provisionally anticipates incorporation into his resurrection) as unity in the Spirit of Christ. We know this Spirit not only as an object of our consciousness but also as a reality within which we live. It is in the Spirit of God who raised Jesus from the dead that—through the mediation of Jesus Christ—we know God the Father both as the object of our worship and as the one in whom we live and move and have our being.

All this is not said simply that trinitarian orthodoxy may be elaborately satisfied. Pannenberg sees that many of the problems and confusions of contemporary theology arise from failure to give due weight to the Spirit in his distinct personality or identity within the Godhead. Much, for example, has been written about the irreducible subjectivity of God. There is a sound insight behind such talk. God is not an object among other objects. But to say that we cannot talk of God as object at all is, in fact, to deny us the right of any coherent discourse about him. If we can know anything at all about God and talk coherently about him at all, then there must be an element in his reality which corresponds to our experience of objectivity as well as something which corresponds to our experience of subjectivity. God, to be God, must somehow be beyond the subject–object dichotomy; yet in such a way that he does not obliterate that relationship but takes it up into his own unity.

As Holy Spirit, God is the ultimate subject of all experience—especially in relation to the end-time when all is gathered up into God. Yet at the same time the objectivity of the world and of ourselves over against God is preserved; for it is precisely by being taken up into him in the resurrection by the Spirit of life that our identity is preserved.

Thus it is by a proper understanding of the distinction of the

Holy Spirit from the Father and the Son within the unity of God that we are preserved from the errors of deism (which separates the world absolutely from God) and pantheism (which identifies the world absolutely with God).

'The Spirit of the knowledge of God in Jesus is the Spirit of God only in so far as believers distinguish themselves in such knowledge from God as creatures and from Jesus Christ as 'servants' of the Lord: precisely in the humility of this self-differentiation from God that avoids all mystical exuberance, believers prove themselves to possess God's Spirit and thus to participate in God himself.' [6]

Can this whole argument be stated in more simple and summary form? I think it can.

First recall the structure of the argument establishing the distinction of the Father and the Son within the Godhead.

1. As the final revelation of God, Jesus is identical with the essence of God.

2. But differentiation from God is an element in the life of Jesus.

3. Therefore this differentiation belongs to the essence of God. Now consider:

1. We are in essence what we shall become.

2. In faith and hope we believe that we shall become one with Christ in the resurrection.

3. This comes about through the action of the Spirit of God and Christ in us as the Spirit of life.

4. We experience this unity with God in Christ now in a partial and anticipatory way.

5. But differentiation from both God the Father and Christ the Son is an element within our experience of essential unity with both.

6. Therefore the Spirit by whom we are so united in Christ to God is distinct from the Father and the Son in a similar way to

[6] *Jesus—God and Man*, p. 176.

that in which they are distinct from one another within the God-head.

The second argument is more complex; but it has essentially the same structure as the first—deriving the difference from elements interior to the identity of essence.

'The most difficult problem of a doctrine of the Holy Spirit, namely the question of his personal independence within the Trinity, can be approached only from the perspective of the personal manner that belongs to the working of the Spirit in believers.' [7]

Trinitarian doctrine as a form of otiose speculation about a heavenly, metaphysical *danse à trois* is no longer of any interest. Pannenberg offers a route to a doctrine of the Trinity which could become historically and socially relevant. (The answer to that disastrous break-away from the Christian faith of elements which belonged essentially to it, which occurred in Feuerbach and Marx, can only come from such a re-thinking of the doctrine of the Trinity.)

I have already stressed that, in Pannenberg's interpretation, the eternal communion between the Father and the Son is not some heavenly event independent of what takes place between Jesus and his heavenly Father. It *is* what takes place between Jesus and his God as he is gathered up into the eternity of God in the resurrection. The eternal love of the Father for the Son *is* his love for Jesus of Nazareth.

Similarly, the eternal communion of the Father and the Son with the Holy Spirit is not something independent of the communion of the people of God in the Spirit. The inner working of the Holy Spirit within God *is* the communion of God with his people. Yet the distinction between the people and the Spirit in which they have communion is not obscured or obliterated.

The people of God already stand in a specially intimate relation to the resurrection of Jesus. Their experience of the Spirit

[7] *Ibid.*, p. 177.

is anticipation of the end-time when they will be gathered into God. In the Spirit they experience their essential identity with God in Jesus Christ. Yet this essential, eschatological identity is experienced in devotion and obedience to God as the one who is wholly other than his creatures. This is parallel to the way in which the essential identity of Jesus with God comes to expression in his humble obedience to the Father.

On this point Pannenberg shows his keen appreciation of Hegel.

'Through this profound thought that the essence of the person is to exist in self-dedication to another person, Hegel understood the unity in the Trinity as the unity of reciprocal self-dedication, thus as a unity that only comes into existence through the process of reciprocal dedication . . . The Holy Spirit moves the believer to dedication to Jesus through believing trust and through praise in the confession of him. Conversely, the dedication of the Son to men constitutes the content of this confession. Jesus is dedicated to men in obedience to the will of the Father who invites all men to trust in him, so that in Jesus' dedication to his mission the love of the Father to men as his children has appeared. Correspondingly, the Holy Spirit mediates not only participation in Jesus through dedication to him, but also the community of the Son—and of the sons—with the Father. In the vital movement of such reciprocal dedication, the unity of Father, Son, and Spirit consummates itself in the historical process of the revelatory event.' [8]

This points to the ontological basis of Pannenberg's doctrine of universal history as revelation. Without this ontological basis his doctrine of history as revelation would be mere metaphor. In true Lutheran fashion he will have no separation between God's self-disclosure in Jesus and the eternal essence of God (though he preserves the distinction). If God is revealed in history, then

[8] *Ibid.*, pp. 182–3.

there is a real identification of God with his revelation in history when that revelation is complete and final.

God is revealed finally and completely in Jesus of Nazareth, but also finally and completely in the eschatological end of history which Jesus anticipates in his resurrection. The eschatological concept of the end of history is for Pannenberg the true form of the concept of universal history. It is the destiny of all to be raised up for judgement or glory before God on the last day. Then God shall be all in all.

If I interpret Pannenberg correctly, there are two ways in which God identifies himself with his creation. One is Jesus Christ. The other is the eschatological end-time when the meaning of the whole of history will be disclosed as the final revelation of God in his glory.

These two forms of identity of God with his creation seem to me, on Pannenberg's account of them, to be intimately connected with the two forms of the communion of God with himself as Son and Holy Spirit.

This intimate relation between the inner communion of the Holy Trinity and the actual processes of history is reminiscent of Hegel. Pannenberg is conscious of this relationship to Hegel. He is unashamed of it. It would be quite false to call him a Hegelian, however. But the fact that he relates his theology consciously and positively to Hegel is of great importance.

In most modern theology, to say of an interpretation of doctrine that it is Hegelian is equivalent to saying that there is something very wrong with it. One can see the reason for this. Christianity did go disastrously astray in Hegel. As a result of Hegel's errors, it went further astray in Feuerbach. Feuerbach used Hegel's philosophy of the Trinity to identify God *simpliciter* with the human species. Out of this came the ideology which supports the absolutism of both the modern communist and the modern fascist state. This was made possible because Hegel seemed to identify the triune life of God directly with the dialectics of the historical process. In such an interpretation the state must finally usurp the place of God.

How near does Pannenberg come to Hegel in this? As I see it, he agrees with Hegel in affirming an ultimate, essential identity between the life of God and universal history. But:

1. He differs in interpreting the concept of essence eschatologically. That is to say, the identity of essence between God and history is something that will happen (with retroactive force?) at the end of time. It is not an identity that can be grasped within time with the Hegelian 'notion'.

2. He differs in insisting that the distinction of history from the life of God is an irreducible element within the identity of essence. What is meant by identity with the divine essence must be understood from history as the self-disclosure of God, and can be known only from the happening of the end of history as it is anticipated in Jesus Christ. We are one with God only in Christ.

Thus the concrete, contingent particularity of history and the identity of man as an historical being is retained. Just as Jesus does not lose his identity as individual person in the identity of essence with the Father; so man in history retains his own finite identity within the life of the Holy Spirit. Thus he is not a being who has infinity in himself. He is a being who is essentially *related to* infinity.

This closes the door to that development of the thought of Hegel which led Feuerbach to identify God with man *simpliciter*. Out of that development there have arisen the ideologies of the modern absolute state. In Marxism there is a crisis for the individual in his total integration into the state. In capitalism there is a crisis of integration in face of the chaotic individualism of bourgeois society. (This is another expression of the conflict of centredness and openness.)

Pannenberg's doctrine of the Trinity, correcting and transforming Hegel in the light of the apocalyptic context of the Gospel, offers the possibility of a new philosophy not only of history but also of society. It is relevant to the search for a deeper understanding of the relation between individuation and participation which is a pervasive and urgent problem in the modern world. The way we attempt to affirm the personality of members in society without detriment to its unity, and to affirm the unity of society without detriment to the personality of its members, can never be wholly unrelated to the way in which we affirm a plurality of persons as Father, Son and Holy Spirit within the unity of the life of God.[9]

In saying, this, I think I am going a bit beyond Pannenberg. I hope, however, that I am not doing him any injustice. He seems to me to have opened a door at this point upon theological developments of great potential.

He has presented the doctrine of the Trinity in a form which, if we can overcome its difficulties, clarify its residual obscurities and develop its potential, could provide the ontological basis for a metaphysic of history and society. He at least holds out the possibility of doing this without, like Feuerbach, turning God into a mere projection of the patterns of history and society into eternity. Yet at the same time he does not banish the triune life of God into empyrean irrelevance.

I find in his doctrine of the Trinity more ethical power than in any exposition since Ritschl's. It invites us to participate in the life of God by participating fully in the history of our own time. We are invited to do this in such a way as to live towards the fulfilment of all history in the justice and love of God in the final resurrection of all flesh.

[9] Cf. *Theology and the Kingdom of God*, pp. 72 ff.

Chapter 8

JESUS

The credibility of Christianity will always depend in the last resort upon the credibility of Jesus.

The church has always recognized that the truth of the Gospel depends upon Jesus being true God and true man. It is not easy to see how he can be credible as both. Pannenberg insists that we can understand him as true God only if we begin with a recognition of his true humanity. If, on the contrary, we begin by assuming the doctrine of the incarnation—the entry of the eternal divine *logos* into the historic man, or the assumption of the historic man by the *logos*—then he can be credible neither as man nor as God. It becomes impossible to conceive of any way in which he could be subject to the finitude and limitations essential to true humanity and at the same time accommodate the infinity, eternity and perfections of divinity.

As the revelation of God, Jesus must also disclose true humanity. God is the origin and the end of all creation. Therefore his revelation brings with it the revelation of the meaning of all history; and so of essential man and his destiny. Revelation heals as well as enlightens. Therefore revelation involves the opening up as well as the disclosure of that destiny which man, often blindly, seeks in every aspect of his life.

In his action and his fate Jesus reveals the essence of man as involving a destiny which reaches out beyond the available experiences of this life. It involves relation and community with what lies beyond himself. It consists in openness to the world, to society, and beyond both to God.

It is therefore important that we should maintain the credibility of Jesus' humanity in and for itself, as well as the vehicle for his divine office.

Pannenberg has shown that it is important for Jesus' human credibility that we should observe the distinction between the *action* and the *fate* of Jesus. His action is what he consciously and responsibly did. His fate is what befell him out of God's creativity in history. His fate is mainly seen in the cross and resurrection. In his action we may think of Jesus as knowing what he is about in much the same way as any other man. In his fate, that degree of self-understanding is not implied. He went to meet his fate with positive decision and courage and hope. He could believe; but in his earthly humanity he could not know. This is true of the way every man must go out to meet his fate. This distinction can save us from the impossible task of trying to introduce the divine intention associated with the fate of Jesus directly into his human consciousness.

Jesus represented man to God as well as God to man. Though his unity with God is shown by the resurrection to be eternal, Jesus' experience of that union went through a process of development in his history. There were three main phases in this: his dedication to his office, his acceptance of his fate and his glorification by God. Jesus represents man before God in each of these aspects. His representative role is not restricted to his death alone.

One difficulty is that whenever men have tried to portray the perfect humanity of Jesus (as distinct from the divine-human perfection of the Christ) they have always painted him in the image of their own cultural ideals. Each age has had its own picture. This was very evident in the 'life of Jesus' research in the nineteenth century. This has tended to discredit interest in the humanity of Jesus as such. Pannenberg admits the tendency in all attempts to describe the true and essential humanity of Jesus. He accepts it as inevitable. But, he claims, the ideological traffic is not all one way. In and through the projection of our ideals upon Jesus, these ideals have themselves been transformed by his power of disclosure. 'The correspondence of anthropology and

Christology has been operative in the whole history of ideas in Europe since the rise of Christendom.' [1]

It is a task of theology to point out the universally human significance of Jesus. It is a task, however, to which theologians have devoted insufficient attention.

In traditional Protestant dogmatics, for example, the work and offices of Christ are usually referred to his whole person in his double aspect as both divine and human. There is little effort to correlate this with his actual historic existence. The description of the vocation of Jesus in terms of the three offices of prophet, priest and king does not really fit his historic existence. He may have understood himself as a prophet (but this could only be in a very loose sense). The ascription of the offices of priest and king to him is certainly the work of the post-Easter community.

It must be made clear at this point, however, that it is not Pannenberg's intention to deny the dogmatic soundness of this mode of ascribing the work and offices of the Christ to his whole person. He is indeed true God and true man. He is really (ontologically) both of these in the unity of a single person. Pannenberg questions the propriety of the term 'nature' as applied in the formula of Chalcedon to the Godhood and the manhood of the Christ. But he is in agreement with the fundamental intention of Chalcedon in speaking of the two natures as united in one person without mixture or confusion; distinguished but not divided.

But just because of the unity of the person, we should be able to correlate what is ascribed to the whole person with the man Jesus as he is historically available to us.

An increasingly sharp distinction grew up between the Christ of the church's proclamation and the Jesus of history. There is a credibility gap here. Pannenberg proposes that this gap must be closed.

Three main problems stand in the way of this.

1. Can we know enough of the humanity of Jesus?

[1] Pannenberg, *Jesus—God and Man*, p. 208.

2. Can the humanity of Jesus—in all the finite particularity of the man from Nazareth—bear the weight of theological significance which would thus be imposed upon it. In particular: (*a*) Can he, in his human particularity, have the significance of a final revelation of the universal God? (*b*) Can he, in his humanity, sustain the role of universal saviour and reconciler of God to men?

3. Can we think of Jesus as existing in essential identity with the eternal, divine Son of God (or the *logos*) without detracting from his finite humanity?

1. CAN WE KNOW ENOUGH ABOUT JESUS?

Pannenberg's answer to this question has already been adumbrated above with reference to the general question of the relation between the certainty of faith and the uncertainty of history (above, p. 46 ff.). In essence it is that so long as we do not demand a degree of certainty inappropriate to any historical enquiry, we may speak with reasonable and sufficient confidence about the teaching and self-understanding of Jesus. In the main, the tendency of contemporary New Testament scholarship would support this. Extreme scepticism about the historical value of the New Testament records has been qualified in the new quest for the historical Jesus in the post-Bultmann period. There is no question of a return to the attempts of former generations to write a biography of Jesus. That is out of the question. But there is a good deal that we can say about him none the less.

2. CAN THE HUMANITY OF JESUS BEAR THE WEIGHT OF THEOLOGICAL SIGNIFICANCE WHICH IS PLACED UPON IT?

In a sense, the answer to this question must be paradoxical. It is precisely in the fact that his finite, historic, human existence *can* bear this weight of significance that Jesus is shown to be not only human, but a human personality in essential identity with the eternal Son of God. It must be kept in mind that Pannenberg's emphasis on the historic humanity of Jesus is not intended to deny or to detract in any way from his divinity. His point is that the two are not in competition.

(a) Can Jesus in his human particularity have the universal significance of final revelation?

This first of all raises Lessing's problem: How can any particular fact of history have universal meaning? We already know part of Pannenberg's answer to this. Facts can have meaning because they occur in a traditio-cultural context. Their context belongs to them and their meaning inheres in them.

In the context of Palestinian Judaism, the teaching and action of Jesus implied a claim to an authority equal with that of God. He revised the law of Moses with an 'I say unto you'. He forgave sins. He not only proclaimed God's message of the nearness of the Kingdom. He also identified himself so closely with the message that he claimed that the standing of men before God in the final judgement would depend on their relationship to himself. He does this without actually identifying himself with the 'Son of Man' who will come from heaven bringing the Kingdom. (It is probable, Pannenberg admits, that the explicit identification of Jesus with the apocalyptic Son of Man took place in the post-Easter theology of the early church.)

All this does imply a claim to universal significance for his own humanity. He could have been deluded in this. It is essential to the true humanity of Jesus that he could believe these things, but he could not know. It is only in the resurrection that his claim is vindicated.

For the gentile world, however, the weakness of this claim lies in the special traditio-historical context on which it relies. Can the apocalyptic context of these events have universal validity? Without that the universal meaning of Jesus himself is lost.

Karl Jaspers denies that Jesus can have universal significance. The other-worldly character of the apocalyptic context of the life and message of Jesus, says Jaspers, precludes universal significance. 'But all worldly existence dwindles to nothingness in the radiance of the kingdom of heaven. Family ties, law, culture have lost their meaning.' [2] Thus, Jaspers argues, there can no longer be any interest in constructive work in the world. Jesus' earthly life would thus have universal significance only as a denial of humanity, not as a positive affirmation. (There are some affinities between this and Nietzsche's objection that Jesus fails to assert his humanity with sufficient aggression.)

In view of the stress that Pannenberg places upon the apocalyptic context, he has to meet Jaspers' challenge. He is wholly justified in pointing out, however, that interpreting the message and mission of Jesus is a more complex undertaking than Jaspers and those who maintain the 'other-worldly' thesis realize. The objection rests on a misunderstanding of apocalyptic and the eschatological character of the message.

This becomes evident when we consider one of the major problems in the interpretation of the teaching of Jesus—especially since the rediscovery of the apocalyptic character of the message by Weiss and Schweitzer. This is the juxtaposition of two apparently incompatible strands of thought in the message. C. H. Dodd sums up the problem thus:

'We seem to be confronted with two diverse strains in the teaching of Jesus, one of which seems to contemplate the indefinite continuance of human life under historical conditions, while the other appears to suggest a speedy end of those conditions. A drastic criticism might eliminate one strain or the other, but both are deeply embedded in the earliest form of the tradition known to us. It would be better to admit that we do not possess the key to their reconciliation than to do such violence to our documents.' [3]

All previously attempted solutions to this split in the teaching

[2] Karl Jaspers, *The Great Philosophers*, ed. Hannah Arendt, tr. Ralph Mannheim, Rupert Hart-Davis, London, 1962, p. 76.
[3] *The Parables of the Kingdom* (Fontana, 1961), pp. 104–5.

of Jesus have attempted to achieve reconciliation by under-playing one element or the other. Pannenberg makes an interest-ing and novel suggestion in seeking to account for Jesus' concern with the everyday life of the temporal world by *stressing* the ele-ment which appears to be in contradiction with it.

For Jesus, he suggests, it is the nearness of the final consum-mation of the Kingdom of God which gives significance to the here and now of everyday life. To get the point one has to bear in mind Pannenberg's doctrine of the relation of essence and existence, of time and eternity. A thing is essentially what it will become in the end-time in the final resurrection. Therefore its significance *now* is what it will be then. Its essential importance in the love of the Father is determined by that. Creation is not to be thought of as an event in the past. Creation is God bringing our present to us out of the future. The fullness of creation is what he brings to us in our ultimate future.

In this way Pannenberg is able to integrate the created order with the eschatological order and so reconcile two apparently con-tradictory—or at least unrelated—strands in the teaching of Jesus.

In the logic of Pannenberg's argument, it seems to me that it is not so much the nearness of the Kingdom, but the *certainty* of its coming that offers the possibility of entering into intimacy with God through the expectation of it. This is the basis on which Jesus can address him as Abba, Father (the one who is intimately present to his creation now) and at the same time proclaim him as the one whose coming lies in the future.

If we believe in the final consummation and open ourselves towards it in hope, then we see and value all things in the light of their destiny in God. In this way God's presence in the world is intimately experienced. But this is not a presence which is different from or contrasted with his final coming in judgement and salvation at the end of time. His presence in the world *is* the orientation of the world toward the end of time.

This interpretation not only solves a puzzle in reconciling two apparently incompatible elements in the teaching of Jesus. It also unites the apocalyptic with the ethical. It offers a basis on which the social, political and cultural relevance of the apocalyptic message for the present time can be established.

Because of the special understanding of the relation between present and future in the message of Jesus, the ethical demands of the present arise out of the future. This is the basis of Jesus' eschatological ethic. Every man has to be treated as God's own son, for that is what in the end he is destined to be and so in essence is. The present is lived in total concern for the here and now for the sake of the future.

This is the basis not only of the private and personal ethics of the Gospel: it is also the basis of Christian social and political concern. Pannenberg recognizes that it is highly unlikely that Jesus played any deliberate social or political role. He was neither a reformer nor a revolutionary. His single vocation was to proclaim the message of the Kingdom of God and to demonstrate its nearness. But the vocation of his followers is not so restricted.

The question is not whether Jesus in his own life exhibited every aspect of the life of man in an exemplary fashion. The question is: Did he in that peculiar openness to God which determined his destiny draw the whole world and the whole of history into an orbital system round that destiny? The fact that peoples of all times and of every culture, having duties and responsibilities in their own society of a kind that could not have been conceived of in Jesus' day, are nonetheless drawn into the orbit of his faithfulness, is itself a token of the universal significance of his humanity.

(b) Can Jesus, in his humanity, sustain the role of universal saviour?

It should be understood at the outset that Pannenberg has no intention of suggesting that it was by anything other than the action of God himself in his own eternal Son that he is reconciled to us. But it was in the carpenter's son from Nazareth that the event took place. It was into his hands that the nails were driven. It was he who felt the dereliction on the cross. It was he whose mission seemed to fail. It was he who died a very painful death on the cross.

Can we credit the death of this man with such divine significance as the reconciliation of God to sinners without at the same time ascribing to him a supernatural consciousness? If he enjoyed such a supernatural consciousness, secretly knowing the eternal significance of his death and confidently anticipating his privileged resurrection, not only is the dramatic poignancy of the event destroyed; its significance is also reduced. The significance is reduced because his humanity has ceased to be credible and his divinity made to look like a pagan theophany.

One might say that Pannenberg's solution is to let the human be really human and to let God take care of the rest. We are dealing with a matter which was in God's hands even though it happened to Jesus. Pannenberg distinguishes sharply between the action and the fate of Jesus. His fate is what befell him rather than what he did.

In all four Gospels the character of Jesus' crucifixion as something that *befell* him is obscured by Jesus' predictions of the event as a task that must be fulfilled. Pannenberg accepts, as would the vast majority of New Testament scholars today, that these are 'predictions' after the event which arose in the tradition of the early church. They looked back at the sufferings of Jesus in the light of the resurrection.

Jesus may indeed have foreseen the possibility that his conflict with the Jewish authorities might result in his death. But it is very unlikely that he interpreted that fate as anything other than the cost of faithfulness to his message.

There is a remarkable contrast between the clarity of the meaning of the resurrection (viewed within its apocalyptic context) and the dark obscurity of the cross. These two events need to be considered in the light of one another, however, for together they form the two halves of Jesus' fate.

Pannenberg notes that the earliest interpretation of the sufferings of Jesus was probably based on the Old Testament tradition of the rejection and persecution of the prophets of God by a stiff-necked people. The fact corresponding to this is Jesus' costly dedication to his mission. It need not imply that Jesus thought of himself explicitly in these terms. In the Palestinian community his death was understood as expiation (though not in a cultic sense). The fact corresponding to this is that Jesus bore the punishment for the sin of blasphemy while the blasphemy was in those who condemned him. St Paul understood his death as the end of the law.

Paul's interpretation can be correlated with the personal history and fate of Jesus in a fuller way. It was because Jesus claimed an authority equal with that of God that the Jews sought his death on a charge of blasphemy. Under the law blasphemy was punishable by death. But in the light of the resurrection Jesus is shown to be no blasphemer. He is vindicated in his claim to authority. Therefore the law is put in the wrong. Jesus' death is thus the end of the authority of the Jewish law. But Jewish law is representative of the situation of man generally before God (Rom. 2:14). Therefore the cross exposes the false pretences of all institutionalized codifications of morality when their provisional character is forgotten.

There is a certain elegance in Pannenberg's re-statement of an argument which St Paul puts forward with more passion than clarity. But I think many will continue to be troubled by the fact that Christian tradition—especially Protestant tradition—has placed so much weight on what is really a rather artificial and stylized argument. To prove that the law can be an ass, and that the holier the reputation of the law the greater the ass it can be, could surely be done in simpler ways than by imposing the fate of death on an innocent man and then establishing the superlative quality of his innocence by raising him from the dead as the chosen one of God. In giving this argument the extent of house-room that he does, Pannenberg is setting aside altogether that degree of tough-mindedness which he shows elsewhere from time to time.

In any case, exposing the false pretences of the law does not amount to atonement. It becomes that only if it is as the representative substitute for the real blasphemers that Jesus died. Pannenberg finds this a credible thesis. But he sees the substitution of Jesus for sinful mankind as a fate that befell Jesus rather than the result of a policy or deliberate intention on his part.

> 'Those who rejected him as a blasphemer and had complicity in his death were the real blasphemers. His judges rightly deserved the punishment that he received. Thus he bore their punishment.' [4]

But then, 'all men are disclosed as blasphemers by Jesus' cross'.[5] Therefore he dies a substitutionary death for all.

I fear that we must do better than this if we are going to interpret the death of Jesus as credibly salvific in the modern world. There were factors in the culture of New Testament times that made such figures and arguments credible. That is no longer so.

Why a miscarriage of justice (which the death of Jesus certainly was) should, by virtue of that fact, be an atonement; why the suffering of an innocent man should effect anything in alleviating the guilt of the men who deserved to die is not clear to those of us who live with the habits of mind and the prejudices of the modern world. It seems to me that at this point Pannenberg's fresh and original mind slips back into a lazily orthodox apologetic for biblical arguments simply because they are biblical. Elsewhere he does not hesitate to say so when he finds the biblical writers showing their feet of clay.

There will be many who cannot readily share his view that a substitutionary element is essentially present in human morality everywhere. One would not wish to dogmatize to the contrary, but it seems at least to be a much more open question than Pannenberg will allow. It must be granted that the concept of substitutionary punishment and of transferred guilt plays a large and apparently ineradicable role in the morality of children and of primitive peoples. But God is neither a child nor a primitive. Substitution also plays a credible role in honour–shame moralities. But it is of the morality of innocence and guilt that Pannenberg speaks.

---

[4] *Jesus—God and Man*, p. 259.   [5] *Ibid.*, p. 260.

If I may intrude a personal opinion, it seems to me a mistake to attempt prematurely to force a 'sensible' interpretation on the death of Jesus. Let it keep its dark quality. We in the modern world can at least feel sympathy with that. We know the kind of senseless suffering that has no inherent significance. This is the worst suffering of all. If it made any kind of sense we could attempt to bear it with heroism. But sometimes there is nothing positive for heroism to lay hold of. The death of Jesus was like that—especially in the moment of dereliction.

It is a betrayal of that moment to find sense in it too easily. Its meaning *is* its stultifying senselessness. It is in the sheer senselessness of the Cross that we meet God's judgement against the world.

It would be presumptuous of me to try to tell Wolfhart Pannenberg his business. Yet I must confess my amazement that this man who has done so much to restore the credibility of the historic man Jesus as the revelation of God has not followed the same logic in the doctrine of the atonement. He has, perhaps, been too preoccupied with the thought that atonement belongs to the fate rather than the action of Jesus. Yet there were elements of the action of Jesus interwoven with his fate on the cross. In particular, it was Jesus who said 'Father, forgive them, for they know not what they do.' If Jesus was the final revelation of God, and so in essential identity with God, then surely the first tentative steps we can take in trying to understand the atoning work of Christ must begin here.

3. HOW CAN JESUS BE TRULY MAN AND TRULY GOD?

This is one of the most important questions for modern apologetic theology. It has always presented difficulties. But for modern man it has become acute. The humanity of Jesus seems to discredit his divinity; his divinity seems to discredit his humanity.

The timid solution is either to qualify the divinity or the humanity to extinction or else to dissociate them so as to divide the person.

Pannenberg offers a solution of quite remarkable boldness.

He traces the fundamental malaise of the doctrine of Christ's person to developments which took place in the early, formative centuries of Christian doctrine. He reminds us that the formula about the true divinity and the true humanity of the Christ was originally referred to the historic person Jesus of Nazareth. When, in the fifth century, this evolved into a statement about two *natures* inhering in one subject (*hypostasis*), the subject was thought of as the eternal Son of God (or *logos*), whose identity with Jesus of Nazareth had become problematic.

It is a truthful caricature of the christological controversies of the early church to characterize it as a debate between the theological school of Antioch and that of Alexandria. The Antiochenes were determined to preserve the true humanity of Jesus—even at the expense of his identity with the eternal Son or Word of the Father. The Alexandrians were determined to preserve Jesus' unity with the eternal Son or Word of God— even at the expense of his humanity.

Pannenberg's solution is that there is only one subject of whatever attributes one may care to bestow upon God's Son. He is the man Jesus of Nazareth. (At least this is what he seems to me to be saying most of the time. There are, however, some qualifications of this to which I shall refer later.)

'It is a fundamental presupposition of the formula of the true Godhood and true manhood of Jesus that it is describing one and the same person, the man Jesus of Nazareth, from different points of view.' [6]

We have already seen what this means for the doctrine of the Trinity. We now have to see what it means for Jesus Christ and the doctrine of the two natures in him.

The position which Pannenberg takes up is essentially Lutheran. The finite, historic man is conceived as capable of unbroken identity with the eternal Son of God so that there is no divine remainder which is not included in the identity of Jesus.

[6] Cf. *Ibid.*, p. 284. I have preferred my own translation here since this reference seems needlessly obscure. See *Grundzüge der Christologie*, Gütersloher Verlaghaus, Gerd Mohn, 1964.

The solution which was favoured in antiquity and established in tradition is different. It takes the subject of both divine and human attributes to be the divine, eternal Son of God rather than the man Jesus. The humanity of the man Jesus is 'impersonal' humanity taken up into the eternal identity of the *logos* or Son (enhypostatic union).

The traditional solution has served to keep the fundamental problem at bay rather than solve it. The problem is always ultimately that of the credibility of a man who is alleged to be also the eternal Son of God 'begotten before all worlds, begotten not made . . .'.

Pannenberg is certainly correct in maintaining that the traditional solution has become less convincing as the concept of personality had developed. Classical antiquity did not have the idea of personality as we have it. It did not distinguish between individuality and personality. In Pannenberg's well-argued view it is out of the disclosure of the triune nature of God and the divine-human personality of the Christ that our concept of personality has developed.

It was in St Augustine's elaboration of the doctrine of the Trinity, Pannenberg claims, that personality was recognized as something whose essence is constituted not from within itself but by the relation in which it stands to what is beyond itself.

That is to say, the centredness of personality is constituted and preserved not from within, by closing the circumference of the self. It is constituted by openness towards the other who gives us our personality in acknowledgement and communion. This is consummated in openness to God.

In the record of Jesus' communion with God, there is no reference to his communion with a divine Son of God. Pannenberg rightly makes much of the fact that his communion is with the Father. It consists in perfect openness towards God. This expresses itself in identification with his message and dedication to the point of death upon the cross. In the resurrection his trust is vindicated. The centredness of his person is established in eternity, not in spite of, but because of his openness to God.

This is the ultimate disclosure of the dialectical structure of personal identity.

Jesus is thus exhibited in his eternal identity with the Son, who is the eternal correlate of God's fatherhood.

In this way the identity of the man Jesus with the eternal Son of God is conceived in terms which are compatible with his true humanity.

This is very attractive. But it contains a great many difficulties. One could easily run away with the impression that Jesus' sonship is purely psychological. This is not Pannenberg's intention. The identity of Jesus with the eternal Son of God is not a simple, direct identity. This would, in fact, destroy the credibility of his true humanity as well as his true divinity. A purely psychological account of the eternal divine sonship of Jesus in terms of his experience of communion with God would not do justice to the 'truly' in 'truly man, truly God'. Here 'truly' means *really* and truly. Jesus Christ is *really* (ontologically) both the uncreated Son of God and the man born in Nazareth. Pannenberg is quite clear that he must preserve all the sharpness of this distinction within the unity.

> 'One must unavoidably distinguish between Jesus' eternal Sonship and his human being that began at a particular point in time. The inescapability of this distinction justifies all the efforts in the history of Christian theology to assert the unity of what is so distinguished, without losing the difference between the *vere deus* and the *vere homo*.' [7]

How does this insistence on the real, ontological distinction between the creaturely humanity of Jesus and the divinity of eternal Son square with the sentence quoted above: 'The formula of the true Godhood and true manhood of Jesus describes 'the same person, the man Jesus of Nazareth, from different points of view'? Surely something more than different points of view is involved.

[7] *Jesus—God and Man*, p. 325.

I do not think that Pannenberg ever quite resolves this tension. (But his argument is of such novelty and subtlety at this point that I may be missing something.) I do not think that he claims to give an account of Jesus in which this fundamental tension is eliminated. His point is rather that the tension between our understanding of the divinity and the humanity of Jesus contains the whole mystery of the Kingdom of God. It will be finally resolved only in the resurrection of the dead when 'we shall know even as we are known'.

But in the meantime the relation between God and man in Jesus Christ is to be understood as something more intimate than the metaphysical synthesis of disparate substances or natures. It is to be understood dialectically in a way which has something to do with the dialectical structure of personality. It is to be understood in the light of Jesus' personal experience of the fatherhood of God; but not in terms of that experience considered in and by itself. It is to be understood in the light of that experience as it is qualified by the resurrection and so taken up by God into his own finality.

In this respect Jesus' relation to God is unique and incomparable. We can share in it only through communion with him and in the hope of resurrection.

In this area Pannenberg has put forward suggestions which are theologically exciting and apologetically effective. But to work them out with the care and precision appropriate to their importance would require a much more carefully elaborated metaphysic than is at present available to Pannenberg. In his essays on the nature of God, the relation of time and eternity, the relation of essence and the end-time of God, the nature of truth, and historical and theological hermeneutic, hints have been thrown out as to the lines along which such a new metaphysic needs to be developed and tried out in intellectual experiment. What we have in Pannenberg is the outline of a philosophical and theological task that has still to be done rather than a finished result. Like the gospel which it seeks to interpret Pannenberg's theology *in via* is as demanding of effort as it is promising.

Chapter 9

CONCLUSION

Wolfhart Pannenberg is best known for the fact that he has restored historical study and research to a place of honour within theology. He has done this in a remarkably thorough-going way.

This has come about at a time when such a move is of strategic importance. Theology has been retreating into a ghetto situation. It has felt obliged to do so through embarrassment over the relation of the special presuppositions of faith and the critical, questioning character of autonomous reason. Critical history appeared to be the spearhead of this threat.

There is a basic honesty in the position to which Pannenberg commits himself. There is only one way to settle questions of historical fact. One must use the best-known methods of historical enquiry. There is no other method which is either honest or convincing.

But what Pannenberg has suggested is no mere capitulation to the historians. There would be little interest or originality in that. What is proposed amounts rather to a mutual transformation of both theology and history. In seeking a meaning inherent in events and in reviving the concept of universal history and of a metaphysic of history, Pannenberg brings traditional philosophy back into the picture as well. History, philosophy and theology ought to belong together. That they have gone their separate ways has not been of lasting benefit to any of them.

In particular, the abandonment of the great philosophies of history such as those of Hegel, Marx, Dilthey, Troeltsch and others as theologically irrelevant has been a severe impoverishment. The cross-fertilization of historical, philosophical and theological disciplines which such studies engendered is indispensable to the development of all three. In their isolation, history has become positivist; philosophy has become empty and formal; theology has become either subjectivist or authoritarian.

One result of this is that theology is left without any adequate systematic basis on which to engage in the all-important Christian-Marxist dialogue.

Pannenberg's success in bringing all three disciplines back to an effective degree of co-operation is of strategic importance—not merely for theology, but for human culture generally.

He does this, without for a moment suggesting that theology is about anything other than God in his divine, transcendent majesty. It arises from the conviction that it is God, not man, who is the ultimate bearer of history. (This is how Pannenberg avoids the *impasse* of relativism in which E. Troeltsch ended up.) God is lord of history and the decree of his lordship is directed towards the fulfilment of humanity. Therefore the whole mission and vocation of the church is not in and for herself. It is directed towards humanity in its ultimate fulfilment, when humanity will finally be seen in its eternal essence as the disclosure of the glory of God.

Therefore *because* theology is about God it is also about the meaning and destiny of man and society. It is the ultimate hermeneutic of human life and culture.

It is intended as no detraction from Pannenberg's remarkably fresh and original achievements in theology if I say that it is essentially as the inventor of a programme of work rather than as the author of a fully elaborated system of theology that he is significant. This is so partly because Pannenberg is still in his early forties and so in the early days of his working life. But also, Pannenberg's approach to theology signals the end of the age of the great 'prima donnas' in theology—the age of the multi-volume monograph in which a whole system of theology was elaborated as the achievement of an individual.

Wolfhart Pannenberg

It is significant that Pannenberg tends to work in association with a team of scholars. Modern theology, if it is to be done in the integrated way proposed by Pannenberg, requires the co-operation of experts in a variety of fields. No man can be wholly professional in his competence in the fields of history, philosophy, dogmatics, philology, and so on, when these are all integrated in the service of theology.

There would be no sense in using Pannenberg's name as a label for a fixed and identifiable school of thought. Theology is conceived by him as being always *in via*. The final truth will be disclosed only in the end-time. Therefore his theology is infinitely corrigible. Much of it has been sketched out only very roughly. The detailed elaboration and clarification of his proposed solutions will require the co-operative efforts of a generation of scholars.

What, for example, does Pannenberg mean by 'resurrection'? This is one of the key questions. He certainly regards the Easter appearances and the empty tomb as public events. But he warns at the same time that all our talk of resurrection must, in the nature of the case, be symbolic. Further clarification of this is needed. If our ignorance of the nature of life beyond death is as profound as Pannenberg suggests, then I must ask the question: 'What, if anything, am I asserting when I say that Jesus is risen from the dead? What would have to be the case in order to make it true?'

In the background to questions about the logical status of symbolic talk of the risen Christ and other transcendental themes, there lies a distinction which Pannenberg derived from his old teacher, Edmund Schlink. This is the distinction between kerygmatic and doxological statements. Kerygmatic statements refer to earthly events understood as acts of God. Doxological statements, on the other hand, speak of God's eternal essence. [1] They are to be understood in relation to devotion and worship.

'While in kerygmatic statements the "I" of the witness

[1] Pannenberg, *Jesus—God and Man*, p. 184

134

expressly appears and vouches for the truth that is witnessed to, in the doxological statement the "I" who speaks disappears. For such a statement only the divine content comes into view. This "objectivity" is associated with the fact that doxology is essentially worship.'[2]

This is a distinction of profound importance. It certainly places a finger on a distinction which is fundamental for Judaeo-Christian religious discourse. Whether it has correctly character-ized that distinction is a more open question. It requires further clarification before one can be certain that there is not an element of unconscious, logical sleight-of-hand at the heart of Pannen-berg's theology here. The final outworking of such an analytic clarification would involve an integration of the functionalist and the verificationist theories of the nature and meaning of religious language.

In this respect Pannenberg's theological position not only requires the services of analytical philosophy; it positively invites it. This is of strategic importance. One of the unfortunate aspects of the rich creativity of theologians of continental Europe during this century has been their failure to establish any kind of communication with the more empirical, critical traditions of Anglo-Saxon philosophy—particularly the various philosophies of linguistic analysis.

Pannenberg has some points of contact with the spirit and techniques of modern Anglo-Saxon philosophy. Such an en-counter would not leave Pannenberg's positions unmodified and certainly not unquestioned. But it would be possible and perhaps fruitful in outcome. Needless to say I do not think that the crypto-positivism of modern Anglo-Saxon philosophies would come away unscathed either.

A good deal of Pannenberg's very careful work on theological and historical hermeneutics [3] has the character of logical analysis.

[2] *Ibid.*
[3] See especially 'Hermeneutic and Universal History' and 'On Historical and Theolo-gical Hermeneutic', *Basic Questions in Theology*, Vol. I, pp. 96–181. This is an aspect of Pannenberg's work which I have treated only indirectly and by implication. It does not lend itself to summary exposition.

There is a basic empiricism in his account of kerygmatic theology. The truth of kerygmatic statements is a matter of evidence. Even doxological statements depend for their truth on evidence which, though not available within this world of space and time, may be thought of as becoming available at the end of time.

But this raises the deepest problem of Pannenberg's theology. How are we to understand this concept of the eschatological end-time of God's final judgement and the manifestation of his glory? Inevitably descriptions of this key concept slip from unequivocal to equivocal uses of language. A lot of historical as well as logical analysis still needs to be done here. Since so much weight is placed on inter-Testamental apocalyptic ideas, Pannenberg's argument calls for a much more detailed and continuing study of what the *various* apocalyptic ideas in circulation at the time of Jesus meant for the *various* groups who entertained them. But this is not necessarily Pannenberg's own responsibility. It is a task for the co-operative work of historians and exegetes.

In all these respects Pannenberg's work is indefinitely extensible and reformable. His suggestions seldom represent a position which we must either accept or reject. They are rather invitations to pursue the investigation further; to improve or modify what has already been achieved. This fits well with his basic theory of theological truth as something that is never final till the last day of time. Until then, truth has its own development and its own history. It is in this sense that Pannenberg is the initiator of a programme of theological work rather than the designer of a finished system.

It would not, I think, be unfair to describe Pannenberg's as a theology in search of a metaphysic. This arises partly from the fact that he tries to make history do too much for him. He tries to make history settle metaphysical questions. For example, it is by giving an *historical* account of the relations between Hebrew and Greek elements in the thought of the early church that he attempted to show their relative merits and deficiencies as *metaphysical* systems.

Ontology and metaphysics must stand on their own feet. Pannenberg has made much of the fact that the only honest and satisfactory way to settle questions of historical fact is by historical reasoning. It must equally be asserted that the only way to establish the validity or truth of a metaphysical system is by the appropriate kind of philosophical reasoning. Such reasoning does have some historical qualities. It aims at what is universal, permanent and categorical in our experience rather than at the particular, passing event.

This tension between the systematic and the historical elements in our thinking is not an accident of history. It is not a matter of 'the Hebrew mind' in encounter with 'the Greek mind' as Pannenberg is apt to suggest. It is a permanent and fundamental tension within finite reason. It involves all the traditional metaphysical problems of the relation of identity and change, of singular and universal, of particular and general, of knowledge and its object, of self and world, of time and eternity, of the soul and its experience. There is a largely non-historical job of metaphysical thinking to be done. It needs to go hand in hand with Pannenberg's historical theology.

Pannenberg's strictures on most of the traditional metaphysical substructures of Christian doctrine are largely justified. Most metaphysical systems have been so preoccupied with the permanent and changeless that they had to regard history as a mere epiphenomenon—as mere appearance divorced from the reality. We need a metaphysical system which can accommodate the novel, the contingent and the creative in history; and one which can accommodate the personal, the unpredictable and the historically active in God.

Pannenberg sees clearly what is needed. He poses the problem with insight and wit. But he has not provided the answer—not at least in a form which we can simply accept passively. History alone, no matter how perceptively it is studied, will not provide the answer. It requires also systematic, philosophical thinking.

These two—history and philosophy—can come together under the rubric of universal history. Pannenberg has given a most significant lead in taking us back to that point and tying this in with a new validation of the apocalyptic context of the Christian message. But if history and metaphysics are to meet again usefully on this old meeting-ground which has been freshly prepared for them, neither may come empty handed. The metaphysician must do his proper job and the historian must do his.

Perhaps something like the kind of metaphysic that Pannenberg's system of theology requires is suggested by 'Process Philosophy' as it has emerged—mainly in the United States of America— from the metaphysics of A. N. Whitehead. Pannenberg has spoken hopefully about this.

In all deference, however, I am inclined to think that a marriage between Pannenberg's theology of revelation as history and a suitably modified version of Whitehead's philosophy of reality as process is not likely to be very fruitful. The similarities are superficial; the differences are decisive. Whitehead's concepts are largely derived from and modelled upon those of natural science. They are different in both ethos and structure from those of Pannenberg, who derives them from history and eschatology. Process for Whitehead is conceived in causal rather than dialectical terms.

The philosopher to whom Pannenberg refers more than any other is G. W. F. Hegel. He is the one who came nearest to uniting historical, metaphysical and theological disciplines in a single study. Pannenberg has made it clear that Hegel's closed system will not do. But the Hegelian dialectic still has an ongoing history in the world. The resemblance to Hegel may diminish with each generation, but it is in this metaphysical lineage rather than that of A. N. Whitehead that the true fellow labourers in Pannenberg's theological vineyard are likely to be found.

BIBLIOGRAPHY

WORKS BY W. PANNENBERG CURRENTLY AVAILABLE IN ENGLISH TRANSLATION

I *Books*

Revelation as History, ed. W. Pannenberg, tr. D. Granskou and E. Quinn (Sheed and Ward, London and Sydney, 1969).

What is Man?, tr. Duane A. Priebe (Fortress Press, Philadelphia, 1970).

Jesus—God and Man, tr. Lewis L. Wilkins and Duane Priebe (S.C.M. Press, London, 1968, and Westminster Press, Philadelphia, 1968).

Basic Questions in Theology, Vols. I–III, tr. George H. Kehm (S.C.M. Press, London and Fortress Press, Philadelphia, 1970 to 1973).

Theology and the Kingdom of God, ed. R. J. Neuhaus (Westminster Press, Philadelphia, 1971).

Spirit, Faith and Church, by W. Pannenberg, Avery Dulles, S. J., and Carl E. Braaten (Westminster Press, Philadelphia, 1971).

Theology as History, ed. James M. Robinson and John B. Cobb, Jr, with focal essay by W. Pannenberg (Harper & Row, New York, Evanston and London, 1967).

The Apostles' Creed, tr. Margaret Kohl (S.C.M. Press, London, 1972).

II *Articles*

Some articles in English:

'Appearance as the Arrival of the Future', *Journal of the American Academy of Religion*, Vol. XXXV, No. 2, pp. 107–18, 1967; reprinted in *New Theology No. 5*, ed. M. E. Marty and D. G. Peerman (Macmillan, New York, 1968).

'The Kingdom of God and the Foundation of Ethics', *Una Sancta*, Vol. 25, No. 2, 1968.

'A Dialogue on Christ's Resurrection', *Christianity Today*, Vol. XII, No. 14, April 1968.

Wolfhart Pannenberg

'Can Christianity do without Eschatology?' in *The Christian Hope* (SPCK Theological Collection 13, London, 1970).

'The Doctrine of the Spirit and the Task of a Theology of Nature'. *Theology*, Vol. LXXV, No. 619, January 1972.

III There are important discussions of Pannenberg's theology of history in:

Carl E. Braaten, *History and Hermeneutics*, New Directions in Theology Today, Vol. II (Lutterworth, London, 1968).

James M. Robinson and John B. Cobb, Jr, *Theology as History*, New Frontiers in Theology (Harper & Row, New York, 1967).

Index